To Judy - With Love and Light
Betty Hudson

Unconditional Love

A Course in Multidimensional Transformation

Channeled Lessons from The Ascended Masters

by BETTY HUDSON

PATTERSON PRESS INTERNATIONAL
LOS ANGELES, CALIFORNIA

Published by Patterson Press International, a division of Global Interactive Marketing,Ltd., 1888 Century Park East, Suite 1900, Los Angels, California 90067 (1-310-284-3209).

ISBN 0-9648317-1-6

Kirk Golding, Editor-in-Chief

Edited by:
Dorothy Golding and Karl Hofheinz

Cover by:

Computer Design by James Colbert
-Bon Colbert Computer Design/Graphics-

ABOUT THE ARTIST

ROSA PIRAN de IBANEZ-MARTIN

Rosa was born in Buenos Aires and studied drawing and fine arts in Argentina, London, and Spain. The main concentration of her life's work has been in sculpture and watercolor... mostly portraiture. At one point in her career, she particularly loved doing portraits of famous writers in Spain and Argentina.

She has spent over 29 years of her life as a sculptress in conjunction with a busy life that includes her marriage to the the Consulate General of Spain, Victor Ibanez-Martin and rearing a family of five children.. .3 boys and 2 girls. Her daughters have already followed in their mother's artistic footsteps. Her son, Jose, wants to be a sculptor as well. Artistic and creative genes run in their family.

Her life is full, and she is devoted to her husband and family. Rosa is truly fascinated with love. . unconditional love... it's emotion... it's form. . .and the portrayal of the two in her life as shown by her work. As a sculptress, she feels that she gives herself and her emotion fully to her work.. her beauty from within her heart, mind and soul are exemplified outwardly in her masterpieces of sculptural beauty.

ENLIGHTENMENT, her most recent piece of sculpture is featured on the front cover of this book dedicated to Unconditional Love.

Here she projects the soul's yearning for self knowledge through reading.. like nourishment for the Soul. Love enriching life and the life of all we encounter throughout our Global Society in it's journey toward spiritual evolution.

CONTENTS

CONTENTS

LESSONS 1 through 10:

CONTENTS

CONTENTS

CONTENTS

CONTENTS

CONTENTS

PART VIII

EPILOGUE...

For my family who believed in me. My son Randal Patterson, his wife Lori, and my grandson Wyatt. Most especially my daughter, Carol Patterson, who shared her genius and energy with unfaltering devotion. For my mother, Nellie Smurr, who gave me the freedom to seek my spiritual evolution, love and forgive myself unconditionally, share my love with all I encounter and follow the ascension path to transformation wherever it leads me.

Last, but not least, Lord Jesus SANANDA, Lord Ashtar, Kuthumi, Mother Mary, Saint John, Saint Germain, Archangel Michael, Archangel Uriel, the members of the Great White Brotherhood, and all the Light Workers - seen and unseen - who have assisted me in bringing this message to the world.

FOREWORD

July 21, 1995 5:00 a.m. Marina Del Rey, California

Dear One, This is **Sananda**. It is now time to conclude your book. I would like to address the general reading public. Shall we begin.

This book has been compiled for your benefit and enlightenment. We love all of you and want each of you to have the benefit of a forewarning of the coming events. As your saying goes, forewarned is forearmed. There has been a great deal of fear and panic generated with the ancient prophecies of the coming end times. Much speculation and scientific pronouncements about global warming, melting ice caps, pole shift, photon belt encircling the globe and predictions of three days of darkness. Pronouncements of heavy, foul, acidic air quality which would make breathing impossible have been followed with warnings to remain indoors without the benefit of electricity, heat or air conditioning, cooking facilities, water or general life support environment.

I cannot promise that none of this will happen. Some or all predictions may come about. We, the assembled Ascended Masters who have volunteered from every station throughout the Universe and outer Galaxies are working diligently to prepare each and everyone of the souls now incarnated upon the Planet Earth to accelerate your spiritual evolution. The process is so simple yet so difficult to do. We are asking you to achieve in a very short length of time what would normally take many lives to achieve. Oneness with God. Ascend. Enter your light body. Leave your useless dense body behind and join us in our task. We do not want to see one soul lost.

FOREWORD

The children and animals will be cared for and evacuated. None of the innocents will suffer. We will not go into details here, however, the formula for salvation is contained in this small book. We have encouraged Betty to include some of her personal sojourn through her life and circumstances to help you relate to her struggle toward Oneness.

Please read the lessons enclosed in this book. Apply the Lessons, Meditation and Prayers to your daily routine. God loves you. I love you. We have all assembled in a massive effort to share our love with you and to help you love yourself, forgive yourself, and share your love with all you encounter. Through love and diligent application of the knowledge contained in these pages, you will be ready to join us, care for yourself and other less fortunate souls.

Call upon me, call upon your Angels, call upon any or all of the Ascended Masters who have joined with me to offer this book. We are all on alert to assist in any way that we are needed, Do not be afraid. Fear is the opposite of love.

Love God with all your heart,
with all your mind and with all your soul.

My heart is full and overflowing with love for you. Come to me and let me share my love with you. Each and every one of you.

You are my Dear Ones. SANANDA

FOREWORD

July 13, 1995 4:00 a.m. Marina Del Rey, California

Dear One, this is **KUTHUMI**. Good morning Betty and Blessings to you. I have a message to impart to ALL MANKIND. To ALL SOULS on EARTH and throughout the UNIVERSE. Shall we begin.

Dear Ones. Time is a relative thing. Only on the EARTH PLANE due to the limitations of the dense body, the pull of gravity, and the rotation of the EARTH on it's axis. You will note that time seems to be speeding up. There never seems to be enough time in the 24 hour period to accomplish all that you set out to do. WE in the HIERARCHY with the assistance of our SPACE BROTHERS from all corners of the UNIVERSE and, yes, from other GALAXIES, have exerted compensating pressures in a tremendous effort to avoid the dissolution of Mother Earth. SHE is a PRECIOUS JEWEL that must be preserved.

Throughout history, eon after eon, many Planets have spun off their axis and dissolved after their usefulness had been served. Their dissolution has caused little consequence.

Mother Earth, or Terra, if you prefer is in a sad state of affairs. Her atmosphere has become polluted. Her rivers, lakes, streams and oceans have become so contaminated that marine life scarcely has enough oxygen for life support.

This message is not intended to be one long complaint. My intent is to focus your awareness on the necessity for change to avoid destruction as a means for cleansing. Just as when you make an error on the blackboard, you erase it and start all over again. We want to avoid such extreme measures as we have employed in the past to achieve renewal. We hope that it will not be necessary to stop and start all over again from the beginning.

This is why we need your help. Yes, each and everyone of you who have incarnated on Planet Earth need to make an abrupt change in your mode of thinking and make necessary changes in your daily lives to increase your awareness and focus on the ONENESS of CREATION. Through LOVE POWER, PRAYER and MEDITATION, all things are possible. GOD is LOVE. GOD dwells in each of You. Be still and know that HE is here. HE dwells in each of you and knows your heart of hearts as your indwelling spirit. Turn to HIM and talk to HIM to find your answers. LOVE yourself unconditionally and forgive yourself unconditionally. For there lies the answer to your power and strength to go forward with success in all your endeavors.

WE LOVE ALL OF YOU. Call upon US in your prayers. MEDITATE and renew your SPIRIT. Go forth and radiate happiness and joy to all you encounter. GOD LOVES YOU. WE LOVE YOU. Love yourself, first, then share that love with all you encounter. Look for the indwelling GOD in all who live and breathe and walk upon the Earth. Following these principals, Mother Earth can be saved.

YOUR LOVING TEACHER AND SERVANT,

KUTHUMI

FOREWORD

June 7, 1995 3:45 a.m. Marina Del Rey, California

Good morning, Dear One. This is **Sananda**. You have many directions to go with this book. We will help you pull it together so that it can be published and placed into the hands of the millions who need this information.

We are now approaching the last half of the pivotal year. It has been the hope of the Hierarchy that the millions of inhabitants on Mother Earth can be informed of the very vital procedures that we have been making available for their accelerated spiritual evolution.

We formally approached the ruling governments of each country and were soundly rejected and were, indeed, seen as a threat to their sovereignty. We were classed as hostile and aggressive when we offered love, peace and harmony. Therefore, we have brought our message to each soul living on earth who has eyes to see and ears to hear our message.

Spiritual evolution is an inward adventure. Love yourself unconditionally and find your Soul. God is love and he holds rich rewards for each of you. The end of your journey is just the beginning of your exciting new existence. You will be more vitally alive, joyously happy, more mentally alert and responsive to your inner directions and promptings.

Each soul has their own timetable. The choice is yours. No one can make the choice to participate in Spiritual Evolution for you. Nor can you make this very personal choice for another.

The course of study is open to everyone for the cost of your own commitment to participate in the grandest universal spiritual campaign ever attempted and offered to the inhabitants of any Planet. This offer comes with the Blessings and promised assistance of myself, Sananda, all of the Ascended masters both here on earth and throughout the Universe and other Galaxies. Archangel Saint Michael and his Multitude of Angels are on Full Alert and at your side awaiting your call for assistance. This is the "Big One" - stand by for the happy ending. Oneness with God is your reward and you are prepared to live and go forward in the 21st Century.

FOREWORD

You will be prepared to participate in the creation of a new Heaven and Earth and to share in the joy, perfect health and prosperity of the Millennium. The Lessons in this course of study require diligence and can easily fit into your busy schedule. They are quite entertaining and simple to perform.

Please peruse these Lessons. I think that you will find them timely and even pertinent to your daily affairs. First priority must be given in your daily routine. From the day you begin you will feel the affects of working through your heart and showing and sharing your love.

Blessings to you, my Dear Ones. I love you.

SANANDA

PREFACE

ABOUT THE CHANNELER

Betty Jo Hudson has been a recognized Astrologer for over 24 years and has had an international clientele who have maintained contact with her over the years. She was elected ASTROLOGER OF THE YEAR by the Psychic Community of Kansas City. The award presentation was made at the 1990 Fourth Annual Intuitive Awards Dinner, sponsored by the Academy of Intuitive Arts.

In the Philadelphia area, she was a featured speaker at the Notre Dame Academy Bicentennial Celebration and appears on the Morning Magazine TV Show. Betty Jo was the featured speaker of many clubs and organizations in the Delaware Valley and presented a Fashion Show with Astrological commentary for 600 attendants at the Women in Banking National Organization's Annual Dinner Meeting, at Palumbo's night club.

While living in San Antonio, Betty was President of STARS (South Texas Astrological Research Society) and operated the San Antonio School for Astrology. There she began her research on the effects of Eclipses and was asked to conduct an Eclipse Workshop, based on her impressive personal research, for the Las Vegas Astrology Club.

In the Kansas City area, Betty was the co-founder of the Second Saturday Study Group which was formed to afford an environment where individuals could come together and openly discuss their spiritual experiences and share their new reality. She is a member of the Family of Light Network (where she channeled Sananda's New Meditation included in this book), the Dowsing Society, the Psychic Studies Institute, the Psychic Research Society, and has been a frequent participant in Psychic Fairs and

Investigations of Unexplained Phenomenon. She has been invited as an Astrology expert guest on Saphira's popular HEART TO HEART Radio Talk Show and has appeared on Kansas City TV Channels 4 and 41 to impart Astrological wisdom on various Eclipses, the Jupiter Collision, Transits, and how they affect individuals and the environment.

Her automatic writing started shortly after she got involved in the study of Astrology. In response to many requests over the years, Betty tells her readers, in her own words, how it all began and what they can expect if they are interested in developing this type of telepathic communication in the pages that follow.

* * * * *

HOW IT ALL STARTED

Unlike many writers today, I had never heard of automatic writing or mediumship. So, of course, I never made any attempt to receive messages and, understandably, I was uneasy and fearful of loosing my grip on reality. This is how I was introduced to this type of communication.

About three months after I opened my first boutique, I went to my shop in Media, Pennsylvania on a Sunday afternoon to catch-up with my book work. It was a lovely, quiet little town, which encompassed just one square mile, but, the territory it governed as the County Seat was vast. Indeed, it took in most of the industrial suburbs along the Delaware River between Philadelphia and the Delaware line. "Big business" in the area was booming, and the space program was still in full bloom. General Electric, Westinghouse, Scott Paper Company, Bell Telephone, IBM, Atlantic Refining, both Sun Oil and Sun Shipyard, Boeing Aircraft, Baldwin Locomotive and many, many others had full employment. My little shop was located on Baltimore Pike, the main route connecting all the many suburbs between Philadelphia and Wilmington, Delaware. The wives and families were my customers and my shop had opened with a bang!

This was literally the first opportunity that I had to set-up my books and catch-up with all the necessary paperwork. Needless to say, it was an exhausting task, taking many hours at my desk. When I finally came to a stopping point, I turned over a page in the tablet with my pen poised and a completely blank mind. Suddenly "some force" took over my right hand and it was drawing pictures and writing a message. The handwriting was not my own and it was as though I was receiving dictation. But, certainly much more rapidly than I had ever been able to attain with shorthand, let alone longhand.

HOW IT ALL STARTED

The message on the tablet read,

"Betty, please call Peg, this is Harry."

Being completely alarmed all I could think of was, "Oh, now I've done it. Harry is dead!! Am I losing my mind?."

Harry answers my thoughts, *"No you are not losing your mind."*

I thought to myself, I can't call Peg, she lives on Long Island somewhere and I don't even know her last name.

Harry again answers my thoughts, *"I know, but call Emma."*

Emma was his younger sister who was a close friend of mine, and lived just across the river in New Jersey. By this time, I guess I just fell into natural telepathy and asked, "Why?" (it was just like talking to someone over the phone). He wanted me to give his mother the following message,

"Mother, please don't fret, you will be with Dad and I soon."

Then I am alarmed, thinking, "I can't tell your Mother that she is going to die!"

He says, *"I know, but when she hers from you she will think of me."*

Still very much concerned about my sanity, I think, "Wonder where I can check this whole thing out."

Harry answers, *"Spiritual Frontiers Fellowship."*

I'm puzzled and think, "Now where could I find such an organization - certainly not in a telephone book!"

Again, Harry patiently supplies the answer, *"The Arch Street Methodist Church at 19th & Arch Street, Philadelphia."*

Much bewildered, I just said a prayer for myself and for Harry, put my books in order and headed for home to mull this whole encounter over in my mind to determine what I was going to do about it - if anything.

HOW IT ALL STARTED

After much prayerful contemplation, I finally decided to take the bull by the horns and at least call Emma to catch-up on her news. After the usual amenities about her own little family, I asked about her mother. She told me her mother was doing pretty good but that she was fretting. I chirped, "fretting?"

Then she tells me that I probably had not heard that her mother had a stroke. No, I had not heard. She also told me that Peg was there with her now.

At this point, I finally told Emma about my writing and gave her Harry's message for her mother. She took that rather as a matter-of-fact and said, "Wonderful, I'll tell mother now. Hang on and talk to Peg and I'll be right back."

Peg and I caught up on each family's news until a happy Emma returned saying, "Mother was so pleased to hear from you and to receive your message from Harry. She said that both Harry and Dad had been with her for several days."

Final confirmation to my episode came within two weeks when Emma called me to tell me that her mother had passed away peacefully during the night. I went to Pitman, New Jersey for the funeral of my very dear friend, Marguerita Marshall. I had always admired her for her loving ways and used her as a role model as a wife and mother, hoping in some small way to emulate her way of life.

Before these events, I had never heard of automatic writing or mediumship! This was just the beginning of an incredible sequence of events that changed the rest of my life and started my quest for spiritual evolution.

Today, when someone asks for advice on automatic writing, I always impress upon them to:

First - Protect yourself with a prayer for protection such as the Unity Prayer:

"The light of God surrounds me; The love of God enfolds me; The power of God protects me; The presence of God watches over me. Where I am, God is!"

Second - Indicate date and location.

Perhaps the most important advice I can give would be to keep your thoughts on a very high plane. Spiritually speaking, like attracts like. Therefore, elevating your personal vibrations to the highest vibrations possible on the earth plane is most essential. Highly evolved residents from the other side wishing to make contact have a much higher vibratory rate than we do here. They must step down their vibrations to effect communication with sensitives here, on the earth plane.

Back to Harry. After confirming that I had apparently mentally conversed with him, I deliberately sat down with pad and pen in hand determined to contact him again. I received the following dialogue when I asked:

"Harry, are you here?"

He answered, "Yes."

To further test him, I asked, "Can you tell me about your death?"

He answered, "Yes, I died after a brain tumor or — operation."

I persisted, "When? Time and date?"

First he said, "I don't remember" - then added, "November 18, 1952 at 11:30 PM in the Cooper Memorial Hospital of Camden, New Jersey."

These were facts that I did not know for certain, however, I confirmed later on.

"That sounds about right - I'm sorry that I could not make the funeral."

He continued, "They really had a nice memorial service in Glassboro - Mom was so broken-up - but proud!"

I told him, "I always told her that you had not lived your life in vain! That you knew what you wanted in life and did it."

He wrote, "All but one thing", "I didn't have a child."

Then I wrote, "But you loved them."

He ended the dialogue with, "I also loved you and wanted you for the mother of my child. I thought you were too young — I was wrong."

Then he drew this picture to affirm his survival and his unique connection with me.

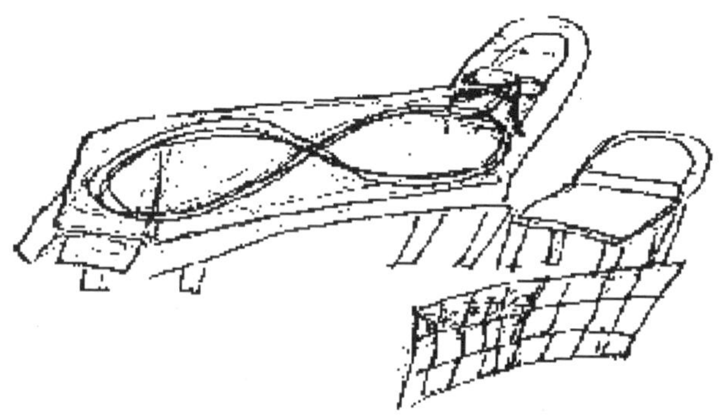

This automatic drawing, that he produced, depicted my hospital bed in Washington, D.C. during World War II when I had an emergency appendectomy. His roommate, Bill, my sister Dorothy, and Harry came to visit me and brought the Sunday paper. They read the funny papers to me and made me laugh until I cried. I couldn't identify the first part as a bed until he rapidly drew the chair indicating that he was a visitor. As the picture developed, he sketched the gridwork for the funny papers.

My sister, Dorothy Smurr and Harry's roommate, Bill Golding just celebrated their Golden Wedding Anniversary. They now live in Pleasant Hill, California - over the mountain from San Francisco.

Who was Harry? Harry Firth Marshall was in training at the FBI Academy during World War II. I was a "government girl" in Washington, D.C. at the tender age of 17. We dated for about a year while he was in school. He was at a point in his training where he could choose to go into the field as an Agent, never staying more than 3 months in any one place, or return to his civilian career. He opted to return to teaching, in part, because he was experiencing excruciating headaches and suspected it was something serious, though he wouldn't admit this to me. He always teased me and said we would get married when I grew up. As a matter of fact, I got mad because I wanted to go with him and he said that I as too young to know my own mind. He was six years older. I told him I would just date other fellows then. And, thus, we parted.

He had done a great deal of soul searching and decided that he would rather work with guiding young souls to become good citizens than to wander from pillar to post chasing criminals. Even though he had always thought that he wanted to be a "G-Man". Before he left Washington, he had confided to me that he believed that to be a dedicated High School teacher, a respected member of his community and, perhaps move up into School Administration would be the highest honor he could ask for in his lifetime. He did attain his goals. His Mother told me that the Memorial he mentioned (in automatic writing to me and, quoted above), was the Post Humus dedication of a statute in his likeness at the Glassboro State University campus in Glassboro, New Jersey.

Immediately after the first transmission from Harry, I sat at my desk daily, in the quiet of my study, pen and paper poised, and was flooded with messages from the other side. The gate had been opened. So many spirits wanted to communicate and verify their continued existence. Many relayed messages to me for their friends and loved ones. In my enthusiasm, I passed along some of these early messages and was soundly rejected. Mortified, though I was convinced of the validity of the messages, I found diverse ways to deliver them to their dear ones. This compelled me to investigate immortality to validate what was happening to me and where it might lead.

Actually, there was very little literature available in the local public library or book stores. But, as though by providence, there was an announcement in our local newspaper that Ruth Montgomery would be lecturing in Media about Automatic Writing. I was so excited but everywhere I turned, everyone I cared about threw cold water on my desire to attend her lecture with comments like,

HOW IT ALL STARTED

"Why waste your time or money going to listen to some kook."

(Please forgive me, Ruth. That was what we were up against. We are fortunate today to have much wider reception to spiritual and metaphysical matters, thanks to you Ruth. Your pioneering contributions and your best-selling books have awakened millions of souls into higher consciousness.)

Resolute and determined to see, for myself, the calibre of the people who would attend and show interest in this subject - that so mystified me - I went to that lecture by myself. This in itself was quite a departure from my usual behavior. There, I found the confirmation I was seeking.

Ruth Montgomery was introduced in glowing terms as an expert, not only a highly respected Political Journalist for our nation's capital and a published writer, but as an authority in the opening field of metaphysics and spiritual growth and communication. She was an eloquent, gracious, refined, and dignified speaker. The audience had been drawn from all over the Delaware Valley. Wide attendance from all of the Ivy League Colleges and Universities - both faculty members and their families, students, business people, members of the clergy of all the diverse religions were represented. To say the least, I did feel that I was in very good company.

She simply mesmerized me by her lecture. Here she was relating her experiences with automatic writing and her initial reluctance to accept the phenomenon as genuine. These were the same emotions and doubts that I was so struggling with and experiencing.

I bought her book, "A SEARCH FOR THE TRUTH", at the end of the lecture and bolted home to devour the contents. That night I had received the pathway to my unfoldment. Never knowing where this phenomenon would lead. At last I had found some guidance in how to proceed.

From that moment on, I sat for automatic writing daily and was bombarded with messages from the other side. My husband was positive that I had taken leave of my senses.

HOW IT ALL STARTED

Twenty four years have elapsed since I received the first message in Automatic writing. It is my distinct honor and pleasure to report that early this year, 1995, I finally met and was able to visit Ruth Montgomery. So many times I have thought about the lecture that she gave in Media, Pennsylvania at that crucial, turning-point in my life. Now, I was afforded the opportunity to thank her in person for saving my sanity when this phenomenon entered and so dramatically altered the course of my life and spiritual development.

We met in the Green Room of the popular NBC television show; "The Other Side". Again, Ruth Montgomery was the recognized authority on a spiritual endeavor. The subject of the show that day was "Walk-Ins". She has at least two best-selling books on this phenomenon. Here again, Ruth is the Messenger to soothe the troubled minds and hearts of these Souls who have been catapulted into a new reality. God Bless you, Ruth.

* * * * *

PART I

INTRODUCTION

Letters From SANANDA

INTRODUCTION

Enclosed in this book are Lessons on Unconditional Love in Action - a Course for Multidimensional Transformation for the benefit of all Mankind. To prepare everyone on earth for life in the 21st Century. It is with great pride and humility that I present this vital course of study, and the accompanying Meditation. This material has been channeled through me by the Ascended Masters; Lord Sananda, Lord Kuthumi, Lord Saint Germain, Lord Saint Michael: The Archangel, and the Extraterrestrial Ascended Master: Commander Ashtar, and collectively, from the Brotherhood of Light. Ashtar is Commander of the Federation Starfleet. He is Lord of the Planet Venus and volunteered his services to work along with Sananda thousands of years ago to protect Mother Earth and her inhabitants during her Rebirth.

We stand on the threshold of a great new era. These lessons were deemed necessary by the Masters as an accelerated and expedient method to awaken and retrain all the Light Workers and Starseeds who had volunteered to join the Masters and work along with them as "their team" in the final days of cleansing and rebirth.

The "End Times", as they are called, are a natural cyclical phenomenon that all planets throughout the universe experience from time to time. Planet Earth is no exception, as any astronomer will attest. There are dissolutions occurring in every galaxy all over the universe at any given time. Scientists acknowledge an expected "Pole Shift" precipitated by the natural cleansing process through earthquakes, volcanic eruptions, floods, and fires, thus changing molecular structures and purifying our earth, air, streams, lakes, and oceans from our man made contamination.

INTRODUCTION

Through the process of automatic writing, I received my first channeled message from Sananda in November of 1992. Automatic writing is considered a form of telepathic reception with the "other side". The theory of "like attracts like" determines the spiritual level of the communications. A saint, I have never pretended to be. But, I have always strived to maintain a moral, ethical code, love God, and find joy in helping others whenever I possibly can.

Channeling is presumed the natural evolution of this type of writing. All of Sananda's early messages dealt with developing unconditional love and unconditional forgiveness. The coming transformation of Mother Earth. And, releasing all negative thoughts to facilitate our spiritual evolution and raise vibrational frequencies to attain 5th dimensional bodies.

Sananda loves each of us very, very much. He advised that the answer is simple. We do not have to suffer through catastrophic earth changes predicted in the ancient prophecies, if all of us diligently seek the God within to release our dense bodies and let our light bodies shine with love and light to all we encounter. He admonishes us to,

**"Love God with all our hearts,
with all our minds, and, with all our souls."**

A dozen or so messages were received from Sananda in this manner until July 1993. I now believe that was when, I received a "wake-up call" and was divinely inspired to attend a weekend Intensive Seminar to participate in the organization of a Family of Light Network. These include four Midwestern states that make up the "Heart of the Dove", i.e.: Kansas, Missouri, Nebraska and Iowa. This seminar was held in Wells, Kansas. Many UFO sightings have been reported in that area and there is a known vortex in that vicinity.

At the time, I really did not have any idea what the subject matter entailed. Acting completely out of faith, I was just certain that I needed to attend. I even presumed to call one of my friends and told her that she would not want to miss this seminar. She recruited another friend to go along, again, completely out of faith. We were listening to our inner guidance - not running off on a whim. There was a knowingness that it was the right thing to do.

A self-employed friend said she just couldn't afford the time or the money, though the cost was unbelievably nominal. She said that she prayed about it that night and manifested the time and the money. We now know that we all had received our "wake-up calls".

The attendees at this seminar were all very loving and highly spiritual individuals who had also experienced their "wake-up calls". The vibrations and energies were extremely high. By our very attendance, the group was identified as highly evolved. We were informed that we had been recalled to be retrained to work with the Ascended Masters that had assembled from all over the Universe to assist mankind at this time of transformation of Mother Earth. We were further informed that we had volunteered to reincarnate on planet Earth thousands of years ago for just this purpose. We received an intensive indoctrination on the coming transformation and the Ascension and Evacuation process, which is detailed for you in the Lessons that follow.

Now this was a lot to swallow and, believe me, we took this mind boggling information under advisement -just as you may be doing now. Trust but verify was the order of the day for most of us. And so we kept an open mind and kept the faith.

We each had our higher selves downloaded and our vibrations elevated through toning and aura cleansing by a highly evolved and dedicated couple from Wisconsin. Their names are Solon and Demanda. We learned that they had been instructed by the Elohim in this very strenuous technique. I have the greatest respect for these two highly evolved, dedicated and selfless people. I do feel so privileged that our lives touched in such a memorable way. Thus, my eighth Chakra was activated - facilitated by Solon and Demanda. The opening of the 8th Chakra was a mystery to me at the time as my knowledge of the Chakra System was limited to 7 Chakras. Indeed, I was dense about these matters at the time. I still have so much to learn and to incorporate my new found knowledge in my daily life. Believe me, so much information was fed to us that weekend that it took most of us close to a year to digest and sort. Perhaps this process will continue as long as I remain on the earth plane. I am still continually receiving and evaluating.

During the Sunday church service various Spiritual Ministers from the four states were delivering messages to individuals in the congregation. Knowing that I received automatic writing from Sananda, my friend sitting next to me whispered, "Are you going to give messages?"

I told her, "No, I don't want to go to sleep in church since we are in the first pew."

She turned her attention back to the service. A short while later, I awoke, terribly embarrassed, with all of the Ministers and some of my friends anxiously hovering over me. What had I done? Fainted or something? I asked, "What happened?"

The Minister of the Church smiled and leaned over with outstretched arms and told me that I had given her a message from John and Mary. Still not having a clue, I asked if she had an Uncle John and Aunt Mary. She smiled and said the message was from "The John and The Mary". They revealed that St. John gave the following message - calling out in a deep masculine voice,

"Evadne, Evadne, (the Minister's given name). This is John, Mary is here too. We bring you a white rose and our Blessings, too. We are much pleased with your service today and the work that you are doing in bringing this group together."

Her sermon was on the Book of Revelations which was written by St. John. I later learned that we open to telepathic communication with the higher realms; the Hierarchy, when our 8th Chakra has been activated.

A short time after this intensive seminar, Sananda requested that I sit for automatic writing on a daily basis between the hours of 3:30 and 5:00 a.m. He indicated that these are the hours most conducive for clear-channel communication. One of the many things that all Light Workers (as we are now called) found that we have in common was a strange wakefulness between the hours of 3:00 and 5:00 a.m.

For some time prior to Sananda's request, I had been awakened at this hour with lovely music playing in my head. This had been going on for several months. I mentioned this to my friend that channels Great White Feather. She has endless knowledge in this kind of thing. She told me to just ask the spirit to come back later. Taking her advise, I complimented the spirit on the music and explained that I would like a little more sleep and invited them to return around 6:30 or 7:00. They did just that and it is truly enjoyable to start my day with Angelic Music. Unlike these musical interludes, Sananda gently calls my name. A wonderful, loving feeling goes through me and I am instantly alert, energized and fully conscious, ready to go to work. It is as though a dear friend has dropped by for a visit to tell me something that I need to know and to help me work on a special project.

Back to his request for daily automatic writing. Sananda explained that He had a series of lessons that He must impart. Each morning, at the appointed hour, I would awaken, rise and dress in my robe and slippers, go into my adjacent office and report for duty. The first transmissions were received in automatic writing using pen and paper. Later in the day I would transfer the messages to the computer. Sananda and Ashtar suggested that I move directly to the computer and eliminate the long transcriptions. So after that, every morning I turned on my computer and reported for duty at the appointed hour. They were always very cheerful, courteous and energetic. Their enthusiasm reminded me of a team of top executives, designers and engineers who had long planned every minute detail of some pet project and had finally received approval to put their plan into operation.

They told me that they had designed brevity and simplicity into the lessons to facilitate activation of the principles. A very powerful, yet simple, message is presented within the first ten lessons. These were so designed so the principals could be immediately implemented and applied to our daily lives. Diligent application of these lessons and daily practice of Sananda's New Meditation promises to activate telepathic abilities. Open our 8th Chakra to receive channeled assistance from the Masters. Release our multidimensional body from our dense, earthbound body, and facilitate the spiritual transformation of all mankind.

In an attempt to come to terms with the knowledge that we had gained at the seminar, all of our group has been reading every book on Ascension and the coming earth changes that is published.

Sananda repeated, *"The answer is so simple.. All the necessary knowledge is contained in these brief lessons. Read them. Do your homework. Recite or sing the Lord's Prayer and practice my New Meditation at least twice each day. Follow the formula and let it happen. We love you and need your help - now."*

The Masters predict no dire catastrophic earth changes or give any specific dates. Just that time is short and is accelerating. The Millennium is just a few short years away. We must prepare ourselves, now, for life in the 21st Century and for a bright new future of peace and harmony through self-realization and spiritual evolution.

Upon realization of the content and importance of these lessons, I asked Sananda, "Why me?" And, Sananda said,

"Why not you? You were with me 2,000 years ago and it is a joy to work with you now. Did I not promise that I would be with you always, even unto the end of the earth?"

At that moment, I realized that I had been preparing for this work for most of my present incarnation. Sananda laughed as he perceived my great "Aha!"

When I survived my "near death experience" after quadruple bypass surgery (with complications) in August 1991, I commented, " I guess God still has a job for me to do, but, I wonder what, when, why and how."

Looks like I now have my answer. It is my sincere desire that all the readers of this book, the Light Workers and Starseeds who apply these lessons and practice Sananda's Meditation can know the joy that I am experiencing as a member of our Master's Team.

God Bless all of you. May He hold you in the hollow of His hand.

Betty Hudson
Kansas City, Missouri
Marina Del Rey, California
June 1995

Kansas City, Missouri

Dear Ones -

This is **Sananda**, and I come to greet you and to send my Love and Blessings to you. Courage my dears, courage is needed at this time and in the future. Continue to work on your Ascension Temples. This is urgent. Cleanse yourselves of all negative thoughts. Radiate love to all you encounter. Love yourself most of all and know that you are "My Dear Ones'. Cherish this love yourselves but share it with those who need it most - those who might consider themselves your enemies. For they will be most at a loss when the cleansing accelerates.

Spend your time in your chosen pursuits, but make time for prayer and meditation. For this will add immeasurably to your strength and to your ability to communicate with me.

Love God and do not fear. We are always near. Express your thoughts and your needs and guidance will come to you. There is a growing need for prayer. Pray many times each day. Many of my "Dear Ones" in the Midwest, (The Heart of the Dove) have a growing concern about the heavy rains. There is much fear, dread, and negative feelings. These emotions must be transmuted by faith and prayer. These conditions are a manifestation of the cleansing that is now proceeding as deemed necessary to restore Mother Earth to a state of balance.

You must be commended for what you have accomplished thus far. Many more Souls are now seeking love and light and spreading that love and light to all they encounter. The Brotherhood and I are here to assist you. Just call upon us through prayer and meditation. Let your needs be known to us. Ask and you shall receive. Most of all - love God with all your heart, with all your mind, and with all your soul.

We send our blessings and endow you with courage and the spirit of love and light in all your endeavors.

Sananda and The Brotherhood Of Light

UNCONDITIONAL LOVE

November 15, 1993 Kansas City, Missouri

Dear Ones -

I come to greet you and bring you a message of love and joy. Cleanse your hearts of all impure thoughts, of all negativity, of all cares and woes. Love is the answer. Love One Another - send your love to all those poor souls in need - Work Together As A Group - all you who have bonded together to form the Family Of Light. You are all very special people. You are my Dear Ones.

We are all here waiting to help all of you, the Family of Light Workers, their friends and loves ones - their co-workers and their loves ones. The time of the great cleansing is near.

Some of you feel that you must accumulate money - your monetary system will not be the same - goods and services will be the value to you in re-establishing your lives. Hoarding is not the answer. Personal integrity, self esteem, love of God, love of all who need your help - do not be too proud - pride will fall - God will guide you in your heart and in your mind.

My message is to Love - Love God With All Your Heart With All Your Mind And All Your Soul.

Please tell our workers to prepare.

Sananda

December 4, 1993 Kansas City, Missouri

Dear Ones -

You are all gathering today to further bond and share your love for one another - to hear my dear Miranda - to share your joy that is increasing day by day.

Time is short - but what is time you say? Time is of the essence when one is preparing for a great task. Each day in every way we must be building our Ascension ladder - I say "we" because "we" - you and me are one. We are building our inner peace and our inner guidance systems - for it is from within that each will be guided toward perfect peace - a perfect place where we each can function for the benefit of the poor Souls who refuse to grow - who refuse to know - that the answer is simple. Just love one another and you can wish no harm to anyone. You will want only the best possible for any living thing. For God, our Father will provide passage for all those Souls who in their hearts truly love their fellow man.

I want to bring my Blessings - yes we, the Brotherhood are with you whenever you gather together. Just ask your questions that come to mind during your meditation and we will give our answer and support. Show your willingness to grow and we will be there - any time - any place. You have chosen your path long ago and we have always been there with you - with the hustle and bustle of daily life and going about your business of living and caring for your friends and loved ones there has been no "time" in your consciousness for us to speak to you directly but we have always been there whenever you ask.

That is my message for today. I want you all to know that I am with you and willing to answer questions about your concerns.

I love you - each and every one of you.

Sananda

UNCONDITIONAL LOVE

December 28, 1993 Marina del Rey, California

Dear Ones -

As we look toward the New Year, there are many, many things that should be considered. Have I spent my year wisely, you ask. How can I live more effectively? Can I love more - be more willing to share - my love, my life, my wisdom? Perhaps the best is the last - "how can I share my Wisdom?" Your wisdom comes from above and beyond yourself. The wisdom I will impart should be shared with every living creature on earth. For every creature should be preparing their Soul "Temple" now - without delay. The time is near and I have much to impart. The story is simple but can be said in many, many ways - but in the end it can be summed up in one word - Love. The power of love is infinite. Every living being can give and receive love - every living being Must Give and Receive Love.

Through love one can receive the infinite wisdom of the Universe - the way to eternal life, health and happiness and make way for the new "Golden Age."

Think on these things, expand upon them and make them an urgent part of your lives. Listen to your heart - let love show you the way. God is always near. Just ask for whatever you need. Meditate on these things and pray many times each day and we will guide you. You say you want to meditate but can't fit it in? Ask us to help you find the time and determination.

My parting words today - love God and pray - all else will fall in place.

Sananda

January 6, 1994 Marina del Rey, California

Dear Ones -

Again I come to greet you and to send my Blessings on you, My Dear Ones. It is my hope that you are all working on your Ascension Temples. I want to send my love to each of you - the Family of Light Workers. Our Father is sending his Blessings to each and every one of you. As you share your love with one another and all the Souls who touch your lives - spread your love and multiply that love - extend it with prayers and meditations. Send love to all you encounter in your daily lives. Love thy neighbor as thyself. Love your enemies so that they may experience that love and mend their selfish ways. Love God with all your hearts - with all your minds and - with all your Soul.

When you are troubled, just ask my help - just call upon me in your heart of hearts and I will hear and respond - your Angels will hear you and respond. We want you to be happy and able to go forward in your lives - living it in the fullest and striving ever to build upon your inner Ascension Temples. This is your receiver - as it were. At the time of the cleansing, this is how you will receive directions of how to proceed to protect yourself and others.

Love - Love - Love.

Sananda

UNCONDITIONAL LOVE

January 19, 1994 Kansas City, Missouri

Dear Ones -

The time of the great cleansing is near. Each of you must prepare - make the most of the time that you have - now. Look to your neighbors, friends and loved ones with love and compassion. Send only the best to each of God's creatures. Help where you see that help is needed. Heal the sick, infirm and weary with God's love and your healing prayers. Give of your energy. Yes, your energy. Build up your stores of energy through prayer and meditation.

Planet "Mother Earth," is a living, breathing entity. She shelters you and gives you sustenance just as your earthly (human) mothers have. Treat her lovingly and with care. She needs your help. She is out of balance - um - overloaded - over-stressed and polluted. Her resources have been dangerously drained. It is not too late to reverse the trend. But do it now.

You say "what can I do all by myself?" Rid yourself of all negativity. Pray healing prayers - join with others who will magnify and intensify your efforts. Do it now! Send out messages of God's love. Include all you encounter - there is always enough to go around. Love God with all your heart, with all your mind, with all your Soul. Send that love to "Mother Earth" - she needs you. Now!

Sananda

January 30, 1994 Kansas City, Missouri

Dear Ones,

As we are preparing our Ascension Temples, please remember it is what and how you think that really matters. Clear away all negative thoughts. Do your own personal "housekeeping." Prepare your Temple for love and all things pure and simple. Love your neighbor. Love and trust your friends and your enemies. Love will literally save your planet. Love is the answer. There is no need for earth upheavals when all are living in peace and harmony. Ah -yes - "Heaven on Earth" as it were.

Let no one shake you from your path to cleansing and doing your own "homework." You can do nothing to cleanse any other Soul. Each soul must do their own evaluation and workout. Must put their own program into action. Must do their own meditation and say their prayers. Ask for personal guidance and listen to the counsel received. Call upon their guides and angels for personal guidance. God is Love! God is Love! Please believe for he who believeth upon me shall never die. So sayeth the Lord Thy God who is in heaven.

My children of light, this is what I say to you in simple language that is easy to remember:

Love God with all your heart
With all your mind
With all your Soul

All things shall be given unto you. Ask and you will receive even the smallest or the greatest things that you require.

Ask and we will show the way of attainment. Food and shelter are necessary for sustenance. The Soul has other needs as well.

"Where shall I live?" you say. "Where should I go to be safe?" You cannot hide - cleanse your Soul and enlighten your Temple and these things shall be given you. And you will believe and know that these things are right for you. Listen to my voice -I will hear - I will respond. I will guide you even if the great cleansing must come to pass. You are my "Dear Ones" and I will protect you.

When you have questions, do not hesitate to ask. This is "my job" - just as you say! I love you all and want you to be strong and happy. Each of you will be assigned special tasks for which you are well suited. You will be given all the tools necessary. You will all be happy and fulfilled as you go about your daily duties.

I will close with love - Goodbye and have a nice day.

Sananda

March 2, 1994 Kansas City, Missouri

Dear Ones,

I come to you today in all love and sincerity. For every day is now very precious to you - here on Earth. Harmony is the partner of love - just so - harmony is the partner of love. I repeat for emphasis. You may have noticed my thoughts come through you so fast that I cannot always spell as you do. I hope you will forgive and correct as any good scribe would do. I know you get the understanding of my words I send to you telepathically. I hope that I do not impose too greatly in asking you to take my chatter and relay it to the Family of Light.

I noticed and do approve of the growth of the local group. And I am happy to report that this growth is rapidly being duplicated all over the world. I do wish each and every one of you - "My Dear Ones" - could know the magnitude of this movement toward Oneness.

This comes to my message today. Love one another and seek harmony among your own group "First." This may mean that one must drop some of one's own concepts of what and how something should and must be done in the interest of what the group wishes to do. This is especially true in regards to money matters. One must not look here for personal financial gain. One must not be puffed up with self importance. The least of the flock may have the most spirituality. This littlest lamb may show you all the way to safety. With a pure heart and a purely clean Temple this little lamb may hear the call and lead all my Dear Ones in the path of Ascension. Some will Ascend - some will stay and provide shelter and safety for others just entering the path.

Inner harmony is important. Know that your Temple is clear and conduct yourself according to your telepathic promptings. God is Love - Love is Harmonious - Harmony is the path to Love and to God.

We will cover other duties in later communications. Always pray. Sincere prayers will transform negative trends, negative thoughts which destroy peace and harmony. Just as stress destroys peace and harmony within, negative thoughts destroy physical strength in the body down through the self- yeah, through Mother

Earth causing stress in the inner structure of the planet when focused from the Multitude of Humanity.

I will close with Love and Blessings.

Sananda

March 22, 1994 Kansas City, Missouri

Yes, Betty we are here as always, we send you love and light! We send your Family of Light our greetings too. We send our commendations to the work within and without that is proceeding. All are gaining in love and working on their Inner Temples. God is love and much more. He is the all in all - both in us and of us. We The Brotherhood, are his spokesman. We love you all and send you happiness and our Blessings.

We are wherever there is a need - physical or material. Talk to us in your "heart of hearts" and we will be there to assist you and to guide you in your requirements. We will not "dictate" what you should do. We will guide you to make your own educated and informed decisions. This is your "earth." This is your time of trial, tribulation and triumph. We do not want to share in your "glory." We want you to make every encounter an integral part of your Soul growth and evolution so that it is yours and yours alone. It is your own achievement. We are all working together and share in your happiness and your grief. Continue as you are and Love God and yourselves - too!

The Brotherhood

UNCONDITIONAL LOVE

Friday, July 29, 1994 5:05 AM Kansas City, Missouri

Greetings, Dear One - This is **Sananda**

We have a series of lessons that we would like to dictate and feel that this is a very suitable hour to come to you. We will be waking you each morning between 3:30 and 5:00 to complete this vital work. This time may seem extreme but it seems a good time when you are normally wakeful and does not intrude too severely with your normal daily activities. You and all of the rest will enjoy the time that we will spend together each day. We now have you on our computer and you will be tapped by many Star People from time to time in a very orderly manner.

Goodbye for now.

Sananda

July 30, 1994 3:20 AM Kansas City, Missouri

Dear One, this is **Sananda**. Good Morning and Blessings to you. Suppose we get right to work.

The Ashtar Command, the Great White Brotherhood and Myself have a series of lessons we wish to impart to your group at this time. This is rather urgent and we appreciate your cooperation.

Dear Ones, it is important that we bring this urgent message to you. The time of the Earth's cleansing is fast approaching. You must cleanse yourselves of all negativity. Create an atmosphere of peace and love in your surroundings. Continue your prayers and meditate. You must sacrifice your usual creative pastime activities to make time for these necessary meditations. Pray Throughout The Day. Repeat the Lord's Prayer thrice to gain more power to your prayer. You will find when you mentally sing the Lord's Prayer that it is easier and more enjoyable. This will lead you into your meditation. We are working with Betty now as our Channel and when you are together again we will come through to you.

You might wish to tape these sessions so that you can have your own copy of these new meditations that we will give through Betty. I will not be the only one to give you this course of study. Ashtar and members of his command will take part. Saint Michael and Saint Germain are just a few who will be involved. You will no longer need to look for entertainment and diversion. Your time for action has come and we want you prepared for your tasks. You ask, "what tasks!" As I have repeatedly told you, your "job" as Workers of the Light is to Love! Is it not stated that God is Love? Now it is your task to spread God's Love - Unconditionally.

You have all agreed many lives ago to be born at this time. Learn to work together in love and harmony. You will find much pleasure in this.

When we get together again, we will answer your questions, and I am sure you will have many. However, your task for now is to prepare yourselves - do your homework - be ready and prepared for class. Say your prayers and repeat them often enough until they can be continual throughout the day. Meditate as you have been doing until you receive the new ones that we have prepared for you.

We love each and everyone of you and know you in your heart of hearts. I will finish this letter to you, my Dear Ones, my Workers in the Light and look forward to being with you at our next get together.

Love God With All Your Heart
With All Your Mind and With All Your Soul.

Share this love with your dear ones, with everyone you encounter. Become A Beam Of Light and Unconditional Love to All - that is your assignment.

Sananda

PART II

A Course of Multidimensional Transformation
Channeled Lessons from The Ascended Masters

LESSONS 1 through 10

Lesson 1

Dear Ones, Starseeds, Light Workers All! We do heartily greet you this morning. We have many, many new things to bring to your awareness. We do hope that you all have done your "homework" as assigned to you in my last letter. There was much evidence of a great new chorus of voices singing the Lord's Prayer as assigned. I must say it was "music to our ears" and gave us much pleasure. You can not even imagine how much I, Ashtar and his command and the Great White Brotherhood love each and every one of you. What a joy to us to hear your song of praise.

We want you all to know how much we appreciate our Channeler, Betty, and her willingness to forego sleep to take this dictation.,

Many of you have questions in your hearts and many doubts about the reality of the Evacuation and Ascension. It is well and to your credit that you should still hold to some skepticism. And yet, you are all now feeling a kinship with one another in your growing love and oneness. Get together often. Meditate together, feel your vibrations growing and glowing. Yes, I said "glowing." We can perceive this clearly. It is a beautiful sight and gives us so much joy. It is likened to the experience you have when you envision a beautiful garden. You till the soil, plant the seeds, water and feed your tender seedlings. Then one day, your garden bursts forth with splendid fragrance and magnificent color. Your heart sings and you are filled with joy and the wonders of God's Plan and the Cosmic Universe. Praise God and share your love with all his creatures big and small. We here in the Great White Brotherhood have waited for over 2,000 years and as the time of the quickening is approaching, we are truly excited and happy. Our days are filled with joy and love.

Sometimes you wonder if you are truly a chosen one and we confirm, "Oh, yes you are!" We hope that you all will choose to Ascend in the First Phase. Perhaps you do not understand just what it would mean. You wonder if you have a choice. Yes, you have alternative choices. You wonder about your children, your parents and your spouses. Especially those of you who have been married many years find it difficult to think in terms of "me" instead of "we." Here, there is no choice. Each Person Must Grow In His Own Vibrations. You Cannot Bring Someone Else Along. Each of you must, first of all - Love Yourself Unconditionally and learn to Forgive Yourself Unconditionally. Some of you will find this more difficult to do than others. When this is accomplished you cannot say - well, I passed that course, graduated, received a diploma which you promptly had framed and placed on the wall.

You cannot hold this for yourself - Ph.D. in Unconditional Love and Unconditional Forgiveness. You must now take this new skill and share it with others. Help others to learn this skill.

With this I will close this Lesson and give you your assignment for tomorrow. Continue your prayers and songs of praise. Continue to meditate on and practice your confirmed skill of unconditional love and unconditional forgiveness. Please come to class prepared to participate.

Go in Love and Light!

SANANDA

Lesson 2

Dear Ones, we have many new lessons for you and they will be somewhat time consuming. This is a warning so that you can amend your schedules to place priority as you must. We don't mean to be demanding, but, the time is short and we have much to accomplish. You will all be feeling that you must brush away sleep since you have been in a state of sleep some two thousand years while occupying your earthbound incarnations. Now is the time for the promised action.

Let us proceed. This is Ashtar and it gives me much pleasure to greet you this morning. I believe I just shocked Betty - but no, she tells me that she felt Sananda was not here. That is well and good.

Good morning to you all. I'm afraid that I can be all business. There are many things happening in the Galaxy since the Jupiter Collision. Really some very good things, as one might expect from that benevolent Planet. Don't let my brusque manner fill you with fear. Honestly, this is going to be a lot of fun.

First, we have prepared a new meditation that we would like you to begin to use daily. Keep up your prayers as Sananda requested. They have a driving energy that is a tremendous help in focusing and clearing the atmosphere. It makes our transmissions much more "static free". I realize that this is a radically new concept for most of you. You have heard sayings like "the Moving Power of Love." And, thought it was just that - a saying. Love is the most powerful source of energy in the Universe. Love can change the world - this is true.

As an example - last year, during your floods. People helping people through the power of love and compassion did what no Government aid group could possibly accomplish. You Are Our Team. We want you to learn to work as a loving group and through the practice of our meditations you will strengthen the Love Power Energy for the entire Mother Earth Renewal Project. Continue Your Lord's Prayer Chorus. Encourage others to join you. Your families, your Churches, your Choirs. Where possible, sing it out loud - go ahead, the more you do, the better you will sound. You sound beautiful to us now. You create a glorious pathway of light. Your Auras are truly magnificent.

Many of you may already feel greater telepathic abilities developing. We want to build the strength of this communication system. Love creates the bridge.

Betty is asking me if we'll get the meditations today. The answer is, not just yet. First you must truly understand the significance of the words that we have chosen to include in these meditations. Many of you have been reading the Keys of Enoch and know that the order of the universe is mathematically based. Every word, every prayer is mathematically constructed to produce a certain power and therefore, its desired result.

Each and every one of you were incarnated at the exact and precise moment that would produce the desired results for the formation of your physical body to accomplish the goals projected for you. Life after life.

There are those among you that are extremely "headstrong" and have no desire to learn something new when you are confident in the positive results, for your own needs, in the system you are now using. We are asking you to join together your power for the benefit of Mother Earth. We understand that many of you have very busy lives and some are even afraid of mind control. That is good. Keep your skepticism. Check it out. But please do read it through or listen to your leader, our representative. Then you will know that we do have a very good and reasonable purpose.

We have chosen certain combinations of words for their energy producing results. We promise that this is going to be a joyous experience. We are not asking you to become little sheep to do our bidding. We want to increase your power and effectiveness as an individual. We want you to be able to throw off your earthly shields and function as the MASTERS that you are. You have been as asleep on the earthplane. This was necessary for you to function and experience all pangs and pains and joy and sorrows that you have encountered this past 2,000 years of intervening time.

Quite frankly, we had hoped that most of you would retain your Master Functioning Skills when you volunteered to step back to the earthplane. But, alas, the earth is very dense matter. Ergo, we got our heads together to hasten your growth process. Time is running short. You must prepare yourselves for Ascension. Many of you say, "Beam me up, Scotty." This we would like to say, yes, we'll do just that, tomorrow. Unfortunately, most will not make it. That dense body does not slip off as easily as it sounds. It is hard work.

Can you honestly say that you have mastered the working concept of Unconditional Love and Unconditional Forgiveness? In Sananda's last lesson, he characterized accepting and fully using these concepts to the hard and laborious work of earning a Ph.D. Have you not had arguments or judged someone else's behavior unsympathetically?

Class, continue your prayers as requested by Sananda, meditate in your usual manner. Continue to practice Unconditional Love and Unconditional Forgiveness. That is your assignment. Do your homework and be prepared to participate more fully when next we meet.

Lovingly, Ashtar
Starfleet Commander

Lesson 3

Good Morning, Dear One! We will get right to work. This is Ashtar again this morning. I hope you had an exciting day after my last message. Good! I told you that this will be fun.

Make yourself comfortable and let's begin. Oh, I see, you'll offer the use of your computer to our group if we want to go on Automatic? We'll consider that since you think it could go a little faster. Well, we're happy to see that you are in high "spirits" this morning.

Seriously, we do have quite a lot to be covered to bring all the Light Workers up to date. We are pleased that you plan an extra mailing to get the ball rolling.

Greetings and Blessings To All My Dear Ones, We hope you have been continuing on your homework project. Though I realize that our latest Lessons have not yet been distributed, it is our hope that many more of you are now receiving Telepathic messages from me as we are dictating these Lesson Plans. I cannot emphasize the urgency enough. Time is short. You must prepare yourselves. You may easily gauge your progress by the increase of your Awareness and Telepathic abilities.

Continue to work on yourselves. Strive to eliminate all negativity in thoughts and action. Work on your self Love and self forgiveness. That is your first hurdle. After a lifetime of negative "put-downs," we realize all too well how difficult this can be at your stage of awareness. Love, Love, Love, be a beacon of Love and Light. Have you noticed how others around you are responding to your Aura of Love? Keep up the good work!

You might say that self unconditional love and unconditional forgiveness are the first hurdle. After that is apparent, extending that pure unconditional love and unconditional forgiveness to your loved ones and friends is the natural evolution. Now extend this to everyone you encounter. You are not encouraged to become Evangelistic, do this by example. Other Light Workers will find their way to your beacon of pure white light of Love. These methods sound simplistic, but, I am sure that you have not found the true operation of Project Unconditional Love entirely automatic. That is not the way with your society on the earth plane. It will become easier with practice.

You may feel that we belabor this point. We reemphasize, it is important. The more love you spread the stronger the love power energy is generated for our use in sending our communication beacon. You and Mother Earth are returned one hundredfold what you send out. Now isn't that a fine investment of your energy?

Your prayer chorus is increasing beautifully. We are enjoying working in the beauty and harmony of your songs of praise and in your growing light. We expect a tremendous increase when you receive these lessons and really get started on your homework projects. We told you that this will be a joyous time.

Notice how you now have more time for your meditation? How great it feels to be about your "father's business"? As you work toward perfection you will feel the weight of all the old worries and frustrations about the "future" rolling off your shoulders. But don't celebrate just yet. There is still much work to do and you must be diligent. Time is short, you are working against a deadline. You are preparing for the Millennium. Praise God.

Now that you have started your personal inventory of worries and frustrations, take them out, one by one. Shake them off, look them over. You've been carrying them around with you for some time now. Lighten your load. Deal with them one by one. Eliminate, lighten your load. "Lighten up" and glow as your Love Power grows.

We told you this would be fun. Freedom feels good. Smile more, laugh more - "lighten up!" Clean out your personal "closet" of all those good things you thought of doing for someone but just didn't get around to doing. "Lighten up," pull them out one by one - inspect them - prioritize if necessary - decide - do it. You not only feel good but you have made someone else feel good as well. You both are glowing with love and light.

Get "organized" around your home and business as you would when planning a long journey. Put your affairs in order. Believe it and act as if you do. Take time for due consideration of all eventualities.

These are your Assignments. Do your Homework Projects and be prepared. Bask in the radiance of accomplishment of a tough job well done.

Goodbye for now. I salute you, my dear Light Workers. We can do this working together. We in the Brotherhood love you very much.

Ashtar
Commander Of The Starfleet

Lesson 4

Greetings To All Light Workers In Kansas City - The Heart Of The Dove! This is Kuthumi coming to greet you this rainy morning.

We in the Great White Brotherhood have anxiously awaited these days of Mother Earth's quickening. It fills our hearts with joy and we want you to share in that joy. You have all worked diligently many earth lives toward this moment whether you realize it or not. These lessons will be a joyous experience for each of you also.

We have come to realize, here in the Great White Brotherhood that our Lessons must be entertaining to get your fullest attention and cooperation without some delay. Of course, we jest but we know with "O.J." competing for our audience, this had better be good! We want you to realize that shedding your dense body will be a difficult task. But with diligence on your part and help from all of us, we can speed-up the process. As the saying goes, "It's a tough nut to crack," but we can do it together.

As it has been explained to you in an earlier lesson, we have devised several new meditations that will help in this urgent process. While we do not know the exact dates of these last days, we do know that the process has begun and Earthtime, as you know it, is short. What you are preparing for in a very short span of time took most of the Brotherhood members many, many Earth Incarnations to accomplish. We need your cooperation to return to us and help us rebuild a Working Team of Masters that can in turn build their own Team in a pyramid fashion. It's all in the mathematical order - as are all things throughout the Universe.

Now, how are you coming with your "homework assignment?" We realize that these things take time and cannot be accomplished overnight. But, with Our Team working in concert, these loose ends can be pulled together in a minimum of time. We are attempting to accelerate your awareness. Many of you do not need this type of reminders. This is all well and good! Go to the head of the class! However, many of our younger Light Workers do. And some of the older ones, too. In the dense body it is easy to think, "there"s always a tomorrow" and have fallen into the habit of procrastination. We are just trying to help you set your priorities. Improve your "study habits" for peak efficiency.

Dwell on this thought - will there be a tomorrow? This is the main theme for my lesson today. Will There Be A Tomorrow? Get into action, you can do it. This is the mission you have been waiting for, these 2,000 years. Hear Gabriel's Bugle. Sharpen your skills and go to work. Set your other priorities aside. This is your most urgent task. Set it on the front burner! Put your affairs in order. Make final decisions as though your life depended on it. In many cases, it does.

This is your Survival Manual. Meetings on sharpening your Survival Skills are well and good, but, you must survive in your fullest awareness as a Master before you can help others. Build your awareness NOW. Set your priorities for building your Ascension Temple first. You must first and foremost work on shedding your dense body. Get rid of all that baggage you have been accumulating these 2,000 years. Show your light and let it glow.

We here in the Great White Brotherhood, are anxiously awaiting your return. We need you NOW. Do not hesitate to call upon us by name during your meditations when you have questions. Call upon your Angels for assistance, they are at your beck and call to help you perform these miracles. Call upon Sananda, he is never too busy to help. Call upon St. Michael, there is no opponent that he cannot master. You know who we are, exercise your kinship. Put it on. Feel how well it fits. How comfortable it is to be back in your old mantle. Mentally test your wings and fly! We love you all and want to welcome each and every one of you home!

Continue your work on your Homework Project. Review all your Lessons and check them off when you feel you have made some accomplishment toward your goals. Make a checklist and mark your progress. You will receive a star in heaven if you are the first to hand in your work! Smile! We Love You!

Good Luck!

Kuthumi

Lesson 5

Dear Ones, Light Workers, All. We are very pleased with your progress with your Homework Projects. We are receiving fine reception to your Lord's Prayer Chorus. The music is truly divine! Many new channels are developing among you. This has been our plan and we are very pleased with the results so far. It can only get better and better. Congratulations and my Blessings to You!

Our Team is developing nicely. When you are focused on a common goal, the results are truly amazing. Continue your Meditations. I understand that you have planned your next gathering. I will be there. Bring your recorders. I will have your first new meditation that we have prepared for you. In the meantime, continue your prayers and meditations. Formulate any questions you might have regarding the Evacuation and Ascension Process. I am sure that many of you still have some difficulty in accepting the concept and the part that you have been asked to play. In your heart of hearts you have a knowing that 2,000 years ago you made your commitment to take part.

At present we want you to focus on building your Ascension Temples and all of its implications and ramifications. Your Love Power is increasing rapidly. And I am sure that you are finding that you are having the time of your life. The preparations and anticipations of a coming event many times is the best part. In performing acts of love and kindness we get an immediate reward of increased awareness of the beautiful things that are happening around us. This gives one the incentive to seek more opportunities for loving acts of kindness and compassion for your fellow man and others less fortunate.

These Lessons that we have prepared for you are not difficult tasks when taken step by step. It is the concerted effort that is the product and the opening of your awareness. Realigning your priorities to make room in your busy schedules for those acts of kindness and displays of love and compassion that you just never quite had the time or energy to perform.

How are your plans coming along for organizing your affairs? We know that the realization that one day may be your last day in this incarnation has not yet had the full impact upon your awareness. No need for sadness. This should be a joyous time of anticipation. Gradually relinquish control. Share your love and your wealth with those whom you love and cherish. Make known your plans and direct your attention to the task. This is your Assignment. Put your best efforts into this Lesson on Discipline and Action. Final plans have always been a difficult pill to swallow. Facing the inevitable possibility of abrupt changes in the order of your daily affairs has struck fear in the strongest among you. Say to yourself, "This Is My Last Day On Earth! What Can I Do To Make Best Use Of The Time That I Have Left?" Then follow your heart and make your last day full of joy and kindness and Love. Don't dwell on self-sacrifice, look forward to accepting your new and rightful role among the Great White Brotherhood.

I will close this Lesson on Discipline and Action. I hope that I have jolted your awareness and convinced you of the urgent need for finalizing your affairs in an attitude of Love and Harmony. Continue your prayers and meditation. Call upon your Angels, they are always at your side ready to offer any kind of assistance needed to perform your miracles. Please feel free to call upon me, My Dear Ones. Any member of the Great White Brotherhood is anxiously awaiting your call for help.

We Love You!

Sananda

Lesson 6

Greetings, Dear One. This is **Kuthumi**. Good Morning and Blessings to you. We were with you at the Meeting and did much enjoy the music and the opportunity for Sananda to address the gathering. He has asked me to thank you. That ring of music and prayerful hearts radiated a beautiful stream of light with a rainbow of colors emanating from their auras.

Good Morning Dear Ones. Our Blessings to you. Shall we proceed with Lesson 6. There is much evidence that all the Light Workers are intensifying repetition of the Lord's Prayer. We are receiving a clear pathway to your area. It is beautiful. Keep up the good work. It is evident that many more of you are now receiving telepathic messages. This is more than we had hoped to accomplished before the distribution of the Lessons.

We sincerely hope that you are continuing your Homework Project. Intensify your Love expansion. Continue to work in Love and Harmony with your families, your friends and especially your fellow members of the Family of Light. Love is our Connecting Link with you and we have many messages to impart with each and every one of you. We want to establish a broad shaft of light that will bridge and extend to the Galaxy. We can do this with the concentrated efforts of our Team. God Is Love and The Source of pure energy.

We are working with your dense bodies preparing you for the Fifth Dimension. When you intensify your Prayers and Meditations and begin to increase your awareness by accepting yourself and loving yourself unconditionally. You, too, are helping in this process of readying your body to enter the fifth dimension. You will enjoy owning a multidimensional body. It is a very efficient vehicle - and, the price is right!

We hope that you now have made decisions and are making progress in planning your final days with due consideration to your loved ones and the distribution of your assets. Only you know what your wishes in these matters will be. Listen to the love you have in your heart of hearts and these decisions will be made harmoniously and compatible with your desire. Do not delay. It is urgent as the time is swiftly approaching for Ascension. We need to build our Team today. We need your assistance yesterday. We need you to take your rightful place among us and join in the Evacuation activities.

That is your Lesson for today. Visualize yourself taking your rightful place in the Great White Brotherhood. Feel how good it is to gain a promotion. Most of you have become meek and dared not dream of achieving such a high and lofty station in this incarnation. Maybe someday, you say, but, - Someday has arrived and you are needed Now! Do not be frightened or feel inadequate for the job looming into your consciousness. You have all functioned in this capacity before and you will regain your skills in a heartbeat after losing your dense body and hopefully Ascending in the First Wave.

We feel that this is entirely possible if you are now willing to work on the "shortcuts" we are devising for you in these Lessons and your new Meditation that Sananda will deliver. Please be there. Many of us will accompany Sananda and be open for discussion. We will be giving this our best effort and we do appreciate your efforts toward building your Ascension Temple.

Please review all the previous Lessons and check off the items that you feel that you have accomplished. Identify your weaknesses. Intensify your efforts. Love yourself unconditionally and forgive yourself unconditionally. When you are spending your time in self criticism, there is little time or energy left for other urgent activities to be accomplished.

Continue your prayers and meditations. Call upon your Angels for assistance in any matters. Call upon Sananda. We of the Great White Brotherhood are never too busy to give assistance. Call upon us by name and we will come into your consciousness and will communicate telepathically. Love God in all of your deliberations and all will be well. Good Luck! We look forward to your joining us.

We Love You!

Kuthumi

Lesson 7

Greetings Dear One. This is **Archangel Michael**. I have come to give a message of Courage. Shall we begin.

Dear Ones - Light Workers and to all those hearts that you will touch. I bring to you a message of Courage. These Lessons that we bring to you can require much courage from you in the proper completion of each lesson in a minimum of time.

Courage is needed to accept the theory of Evacuation and Ascension. More courage is needed in stepping from acceptance into action. You might call this a "Giant Step" on your part. It is all well and good to bandy about discussion of the Ascension Process. The acceptance of the inevitability of cataclysmic earth changes and the survival skills needed to help others who are caught unaware, unaccepting and unprepared for the aftermath of this necessary cleansing. Courage, Courage, Courage. This is what is required of you at this moment in history. Time Is Critical! This is an urgent matter requiring immediate action on the part of all the Light Workers.

It is our hope that all of you will accept this as reality and move to make the necessary preparations for your fullest participation in this accelerated mission. MISSION? Yes, your mission is to live and love in such a way that you can quickly shed your dense body in a minimum of time. Many of you now feel flattered to be included in this class. Flattered to be reminded that you functioned as a Master some 2,000 or more years ago and made a commitment to return to the Earthplane. Your Soul purpose is to retrain to take your place in this time in history and fulfill your purpose.

Like any Army recalled into service, you must now have an intensive training course to whip you into shape for the battle ahead. Heed this call and be prepared to leave on a moment's notice like any good soldier. Curtail your normal activities insofar as it is practical. Work on your "Homework." Any fitness program can be exhilarating. Working together as our Team will be an enjoyable task once you gain momentum. Love, Love, Love will give you the power and the energy required to accomplish these accelerated demands.

My Sword and I will be standing by to lend assistance in cutting your ties. We intend to lift you up, through prayer and meditation, so that I can help cut your ties with my mighty sword. From that point on, your body will become lighter and lighter.

It is our intention to keep each of your daily Lessons short so that you can spend a minimum time in reading and a maximum time in action. Time is speeding up. Ah, this you have noticed! Good! You will notice as you make progress in your "Homework" that your body will become lighter, you will have a noticeable increase in vibratory rate, and your tasks will become more enjoyable.

Goodbye for now. It has been a pleasure to be with you today. Please call upon me. I want to help in any way I can. I love you and look forward to your return home.

In Love And Light,

Archangel Michael

Lesson 8

Greetings to The KC Starseeds and Light Workers. It is indeed a pleasure to Greet each of you and to send this Lesson on Courage and Acceptance. Given more time, this would surely be a natural evolution for each of you. You are Ascended Masters who have returned to the Earth Plane for this special duty. We here in the Hierarchy seemed to miscalculate the density of the Earth Plane and the natural grounding and attachments that you would develop. However, it is now necessary to accelerate your release from your earthly ties. I am quite adept at wielding my trusty sword for that purpose. Do not be concerned regarding my accuracy. My aim is unerring.

Your Lord's Prayer Chorus daily increases in power and is emitting the most beautiful glowing music and play of lights. It is indeed a pleasure to behold and makes our communication much more effective.

Your prayers plus your meditations are proving a most helpful aid in restructuring your bodies through your cells. Thank you for your cooperation. I am sure that you are noticing the increase in your bodily vibrations and the opening of your chakras. Most of our work is done through your second, third and fourth chakras. However, we will be adding additional chakras as we move you into your Fifth Dimensional Bodies. We recognize that you are feeling an overwhelming urge for sleep at this time. That is well and good. Please yield to this desire for sleep. When you are in your sleep state, you are lending your cooperation and assistance in our body restructuring work.

You may also be experiencing various pains and hitherto unnoticed symptoms. We apologize, too, it is part of the process and another good reason for you to yield to sleep. We can work more effectively while you are in the relaxed, sleeping state. One day soon you will become aware of a feeling of fitness and joyous zest for living. Love in action brings much personal happiness. Every loving act you perform spreads joyous love not only to you and the others involved in each loving act but continues to multiply in pyramid fashion. Truly Love Makes The World Go Around!

Surely when you read some of the above, with your sophisticated and worldly wise persona you complain that this seems too simplistic to be of consequence. God Is Love and All Things Are Possible Through His Love!

Love God with all your Heart,
With all your Soul and with all your Mind.

Courage and Acceptance of your ultimate goal and personal commitment to Ascend is all that is needed to complete the picture. We sincerely hope that your choice will be to ascend with the first wave. Experience the joy of returning to your heavenly home and reuniting with your heavenly family and friends. Your retraining will be a joyous experience. Remember, I am your constant companion and I am ready and willing to assist you in cutting your earthly ties. You are my family and I love each and every one of you.

As promised, I will keep this Lesson brief. We in the Great White Brotherhood are all standing by and eager to lend assistance to you with your "Homework" and your preparations for Ascension. Call on us!

Archangel Michael

Lesson 9

Good Morning, Dear One. We hope you had an interesting day. Negativity and lack of acceptance to these Lessons can happen. Don't be disheartened. The power of the Ego is strong among Ascended Masters who have returned to Earth and pledged to help in the Ascension process. We know that this is a large part of the Earthbound Soul that must be released before our Light Workers can work as a Team.

This is our challenge. Time is short. We are diligently pulling these Lessons together to appeal to as many of you as possible. We aim to encourage you to prepare your Ascension Temples Now. Review your Lessons on Courage and Acceptance.

Greetings To All Starseeds And Light Workers in the Heart Of The Dove! It brings me much pleasure to come to you this morning. We, here in the Great White Brotherhood are very excited and joyously anticipating your Ascension. We look forward to your speedy processing and your return to your status as a functioning Master. We realize that the Ascension and Evacuation of Mother Earth will be a tremendous task. However, with all of you retrained and eagerly joining with The Brotherhood, we will form an unbeatable Team.

We promise that you will never be bored or lacking entertainment. This will be a most pleasant task. The cleansing and restructuring of Mother Earth is awesome to contemplate. She is in desperate need of renewal. Our Team will be equal to the task. There will be three waves of Ascension. We sincerely hope that you choose to Ascend with the First Wave so that you will be ready to participate with the subsequent Second and Third Waves. No one will be lost. We will relocate everyone on the Planet. However, the changes can cause much chaos among those who do not choose to accept our offer of assistance. Many loving hearts will be needed to join our team and work together to alleviate the mass hysteria that can occur.

Mother Earth will be returned to pristine beauty. Clear streams, new mountain ranges, blue skies, balmy weather and totally re-contoured continents will welcome in the Millennium.

You will repopulate Mother Earth and enjoy 1,000 years of joy, peace and harmony. You will have earned the right as reward for your labors of love and the assistance that you lend others during the transformation.

Mother Earth is a living, breathing Planet. She was never intended to be scarred by the greed of a few who have created havoc in her atmosphere. Indeed if this necessary cleansing were not completed at this time the entire Galaxy would be threatened. Have no fear. There are many volunteers working with us on this project. We have participants from all over the Galaxy. We have a joyous army amassed to assist. Now, your job is to prepare your Ascension Temples. Let love loosen your dense bodies. Do your "Homework" with swift efficiency. Time is short. We look forward to your participation in this grand and glorious project for humanity. Continue with your Prayers and Meditations. We look forward to being with you on Saturday Evening.

It has been my pleasure to address you Dear Ones today!

Saint Germain

Lesson 10

Good Morning Dear One. This Is **Sananda**. We are happily looking forward to meeting with the group tomorrow evening. Time is short and we have been kept on our toes all over the Galaxy. Shall we begin?

Dear Ones Greetings To All You Beautiful Light Workers. This Is Sananda. Many members of the Great White Brotherhood have made arrangements to attend your gathering tomorrow evening. There should be powerful Love Energy available for our discussions. We have anticipated this type of meeting for a long time now and we are joyously looking forward to being with you.

This Lesson will be a brief reminder to you. Please review all your previous "Homework" assignments. Please be ready to participate in class. Be prepared to take notes and bring your tape recorders. There have been previously published Meditations that I have dictated. This Meditation that I will give you tomorrow is much more powerful and it is brief. We felt during our deliberations that we wanted to create a new Meditation that could be quickly learned by our Light Workers. There is much urgency for our time is short.

Please continue your Prayers and Meditations. We now are communicating with quite a few of my Dear Ones. As mentioned above, this Lesson is just a brief reminder of our meeting and suggestions that you review the Lessons you have received. Betty will distribute your next set of homework assignments tomorrow. Until then -

Love God with all your heart,
With all Your Mind, all your Soul and with all your Spirit.

Blessings and Love to you, my Dear Ones.

Sananda

PART III

SANANDA's New Meditation

Sananda, Ashtar, Archangel Michael, Saint Germain, Kuthumi and many members of the Great White Brotherhood mathematically engineered the following New Meditation as a gift to all the Starseeds and Light Workers who are presently incarnated at this End Time. This Meditation has been so calculated to accelerate our Soul progression and facilitate lifting our light bodies from our earthbound dense bodies. Though we have all volunteered to return and have served and endured many lifetimes on the earth plane, the quickening and cleansing of Mother Earth is at hand. The time is short and this New Meditation will serve as a short-cut to our readiness.

Sananda commented that He and the assembled Ascended Masters found many new channels in our group and that we glowed like stadium lights. With that comment, I have transcribed the following message and the New Meditation from the video tape taken at our gathering.

In love and Light, Betty Hudson

SANANDA's New Meditation

Take a deep breath, hold it - release it slowly. Bring yourself down slowly, down, down, down - deeper, deeper, deeper.

Take another deeper breath and hold it as long as you can.

Release it slowly, slowly, slowly going down, deeper, deeper, deeper.

If this Meditation puts you in a Channeling state, it will be quite acceptable and we'll be happy to hear what your channel has to say.

Breathe in positive energy. Breathe in love, light, joy and happiness. Exhale all that is negative - all that is burdensome. Let the joy and happiness come through. We love each of you.

Once more take a deep breath - hold it and let it out slowly, down, down, down - deeper, deeper, deeper. See the columns of crystals. Clear white crystals. Fields and fields of smooth, clear crystals of all sizes and shapes. Reach for them, feel them, hold them in your hands. Meditate on these clear white crystals. See your pathway clear. See yourself in this light, surrounded by these clear white crystals.

Breath in another deep breath, deeper, deeper, deeper - hold it. Exhale. Feel yourself going down, down, down. See the beautiful bright golden yellow crystals. Feel the crystals. Enjoy the crystals. Step on the crystals, they are small enough and smooth. Feel the energy entering your body. Meditate on the pure golden light.

Inhale deeply. Feel yourself rising higher, higher and higher. Hold it. Exhale, down, down, down - deeper, deeper, and deeper. See the beautiful blue crystals - clear light blue crystals - light blue as the sky. Sit by the water. Put your feet in the water and feel the smooth, clear, light blue stones. Let the water cool you and soothe you. Meditate by the water and feel the love, feel the energy force entering your chakras one by one.

Inhale - deeper, deeper and deeper. Hold your breath. Exhale. Going down, down, down. See the beautiful clouds and mist. See the fields of rose quartz through the clearing mist and clouds. Sort through them carefully. Selecting just the crystals that seem right for you. Pick up two hands full and bring them to your heart chakra. This is the love crystal. This is what you are reaching for - Love, Love, Love, Love. Inhale. Bring in more and more of this love energy. Bring it up and up - hold it, enjoy it. Release this energy, slowly and bring it down, down, down.

Inhale. We are going to your throat chakra. See the fields of beautiful green crystals of many shades and hues. There are many, many crystals scattered around. Run your hands over the crystals. Choose as many as you wish. These crystals have been placed here for you to use. Now find the biggest one you can find and place it on your throat chakra. Feel the vibrations rising throughout your body. You now can express your love to all you encounter. Express your love to all creatures big and small who deserve your love. Everyone does.

Inhale. Bring in more and more breath. You are going to need this to express your love. Exhale - down, down, down - deeper, deeper, deeper. Bring in the bright blue light of the Lapis Lazuli. See them scattered all around you. Feel the different sizes and shapes. Choose just the right shape, size and density. Bring them up to your Third Eye Chakra. Enjoy it. See the pictures. Feel the strength and energy of the Lapis Lazuli opening this very vital chakra. Take a deep breath. Feel yourself rising up, up, up. Hold your breath as long as you can and enjoy this beautiful feeling. Stay as long as you wish. —— You will find yourself hearing and receiving all knowledge. —— Now release your breath and come down, down, down.

Inhale. Take another deep breath reaching higher and higher. Here we are, back to clear white crystals. These are much bigger, much brighter, and much harder in density. Find just the perfect stone for you. Hold it in both hands. Feel its intense energy. Place it on your crown chakra. Now take as many of these sparkling, clear crystals as you desire and create a crown. Wear your crown well. Feel the Love Energy. This is the Christ, God Energy. Enjoy it. You deserve it. You will want to share it with all you encounter. Exhale and come down. Now take a deep breath and return to the crown chakra. Dare To Think Higher. Visualize a Golden Pyramid of your own creation constructed of blocks of

Pure Gold. It is made just for you. Create a door just large enough for you to crawl through and to bring in your dependent pets, if you wish. Upon entering this pyramid, you are moving into your Multidimensional Body. Feel how you are lifting yourself up. You are practicing lifting yourself above your earthbound ties. Stay as long as you like and then return. Wasn't that a wonderful experience?

Now I think that we need to let Betty come back, slowly. Please work on this. Use it in conjunction with the Lord's Prayer. I love you all!

I will say Goodnight,

SANANDA

PART IV

LESSONS 11 through 24

Lesson 11

Greetings Dear Ones. My Blessings to all our Starseeds and Light Workers. It was indeed a pleasure to meet with you on Saturday evening. We here in the Hierarchy and the Great White Brotherhood were impressed with the turnout and the participation of each and every one who attended. We are pleased with your progress. You have been doing your "Homework," I see!

Now that you have the first 10 Lessons in your possession, I want to give you a few instructions regarding this course of study. There will be no formal tests or grading of your assignments. Perhaps open book exercises to self test your progress may be suggested. Each of you will progress at your own speed. Your progress will be self evident as your awareness grows and your telepathic abilities increase. As you use your new Meditation you will feel your body becoming multidimensional as you enter your Golden Pyramid. As you meditate on a regular basis, you will practice entering the fifth dimension. You will know if you have passed this course of study by your readiness at "lift-off" of the First Wave of Ascension. We do sincerely hope that you will be ready and choose to Ascend in the First Wave. We urgently need your assistance. You are our Team.

Continue to review each preceding lesson and make your progress reports. You are coming along beautifully with your Lord's Prayer Chorus. We enjoy the music and glory in the increase in energy and light that it provides. It is highly evident that many of you have now attained the continual musical prayer rolling in your consciousness. Congratulations. Rather than being a distraction, I am sure that you are finding that you now have a new reservoir of energy to accomplish your daily tasks and easily find time for your "Homework" assignments.

As promised, we will keep these daily lessons brief. The lessons are designed to help you focus and align your priorities to gain the fullest benefit in a minimum of time.

I will close this Lesson with a reminder to love yourself unconditionally and forgive yourself unconditionally. All the rest will fall in place as you go through these lessons.

UNCONDITIONAL LOVE

**Love God With All Your Heart
With All Your Mind and With All Your Soul.**

Share your love with all those you hold dear and all those you encounter. Be a living example of the Power of Love. All your needs will manifest and you will create your own following. Lead the path to Ascension through your example of God's Love in action!

I love you very much, My Dear Ones. Sananda

Lesson 12

Greetings to all our Dear Light Workers — Our Team! We were most gratified with the turnout for the gathering and the excellent participation in the meditation. It is our hope that you will quickly learn this new meditation. It has been devised to build the powerful energy that we require to lift you from your dense bodies in a minimum of time. It has been designed to be brief and easy to learn and to facilitate your Ascension practice. By so doing, you will receive the maximum benefit from the Ascension Process and arrive at your destination in the Universe "Up and Running," as you say, ready to be retrained to take your place among the Masters in Service to Mankind.

This is your "Homework" assignment. Continue your Lord's Prayer Choruses, let this prayer lead you into the new Meditation Sananda guided you through on Saturday evening. We, here in the Starship feel very comfortable working with your technology. We are looking forward to your rapidly developing telepathic abilities so that we can contact you on an individual basis. You can do this through diligently working on your homework. Good luck on that, you will really enjoy communicating in this manner.

We urge you to joyously work through your various fields of crystals, visualize examining, sorting and selecting the perfect size, color and perfection of each crystal. Take as many as you desire. Take them in both hands and place them on the appropriate chakras activating each chakra in turn. Take your time and contemplate with each new crystal to receive maximum benefit. When you are satisfied with your selection of the perfect brilliant, hard, white crystal place it on your crown chakra and then you may create your Golden Pyramid on your newly created 8th chakra. You will find much pleasure in being transported in your pyramid. While meditating within your pyramid you can travel throughout the Universe to any location in the Galaxy. No need to make airline reservations on this most pleasant and efficient craft. It is yours, to have and to hold, fueled by Love, for the acceptance of the reality of your pyramid. Is the price too high? It is yours for the expenditure of a small amount of your time. Please accept our gift to you, Dear Ones.

We love you and anxiously look forward to our communicating and working together in this most worthwhile adventure. Continue to grow and to glow. Until we meet again.

Fondly,

Ashtar
Commander Of The Starfleet

Lesson 13

Dear Ones, This is **Kuthumi**. Today's Lesson will stress setting priorities to find time to complete your "Homework." We realize that a multitude of things are competing for your attention. You are aware of the many changes that are taking place in your body as you are being restructured to participate in the cleansing of Mother Earth. You are becoming much more sensitive and are feeling her quickening. The strong desire for sleep that overtakes you can be alleviated by short meditation breaks. As you meditate more frequently, you will understand that the new meditation was so designed to infuse you with new and vital energy. You can now accomplish more and become more efficient in conducting your daily tasks more efficiently.

You are becoming more aware of manifesting your needs through careful and thoughtful planning. We advised that this would be a pleasant adventure! Are you having fun yet? We want you to feel the joy that we, here in the Brotherhood, are enjoying. These are but remembered skills that you earned long ago as you are reducing in density and recovering your multidimensional body.

Please continue your prayers and implement your new meditation. Manifesting is just one of the rewards that you will receive for your diligence. Review your previous Lessons and check each one off as you accomplish your goals.

Many of you have expressed concerns about relocating. Your number one priority can be accomplished right where you are in this time and place. It is well to plan ahead for future needs and accommodations for the many souls that will need your assistance. These needs will be easily obtained when you have regained your Ascended Master Manifesting Skills.

Answer the following review questions in percentages:

Do you Love And Forgive yourself Unconditionally? ____%

Do you Accept the reality of Ascension? ____%

Do you desire to Ascend in the First Wave? ____%

Have you made Final Plans and Decisions and taken Action? ____%

Have you found time to perform Loving, Selfless Deeds? ____%

Have you noticed your thoughts Manifesting? ____%

Are your Prayers and our new Meditation integrating? ____%

Are you receiving Telepathic Messages? ____%

Are you now Channeling? ____%

These are only examples of review questions you could be asking yourself. Each of you have developed your own learning processes. We merely wish to emphasize the urgency of our mission and the need for efficiency. Many need no reminding. Our job is to develop Our Team.

Again, it has been my pleasure to address you today. We love you and look forward to your full participation in the Transformation.

Your servant,

Kuthumi

Lesson 14

Greetings To You, My Dear Starseeds and Light Workers. It is such a pleasure to impart this Lesson of Service to Mankind. We are sure that this message is not strange to any of you. You have demonstrated your Love through Service to Mankind over many lifetimes. We feel that no course of study on the Evacuation and Ascension Process would be complete without some mention of the part that it plays in your readiness.

Spending many lives on Earth before our individual Ascensions, we know too well how dense one's body can become through the pressures and demands of society. There are many, many distractions from a multitude of sources. We understand that finding time and setting your priorities to include Service to Mankind can be most difficult and sometimes almost impossible to do. Yet you have these impulses and sense that you have an obligation to serve in a much broader capacity than you actually do. Service is God's Love in Action. You have a yearning to help wherever you see the need and a feeling of remorse when you cannot fulfill that need.

Goodbye for now. We Love you very much,

Saint Germain

Lesson 15

Dear Ones, Starseeds and Light Workers. It is my pleasure to greet you this morning. There is evidence that you have been working on your homework. Congratulations and thank you. The light channels have been increasing and our communication is much easier. Many of you are now recognizing our telepathic messages. Many new channels are developing - just as we had hoped. The need is urgent. The time is short. We are working diligently throughout the Universe with the cooperation of many, many helpers from all parts of the Galaxy. The Earth Classroom has kept us on our toes, so to speak.

The transformation of Mother Earth with ease and efficiency is the ultimate goal. We have many, many aspirants who are anxiously striving toward perfection of their souls. Working with the Love Energy. Cleansing their Ascension Temples. There is much turmoil, pain and suffering in many sections of the Earth. Mother Earth is torn with many warring factions, starvation, death, pestilence and disease. There is much need for cleansing by the Earth Angels. Many cataclysmic adjustments are necessary in the form of floods, earthquakes, volcanic eruptions, fires and landslides. My dear ones, every Soul on Earth is in peril. It is necessary to awaken your consciousness to the urgency of your role you have volunteered to play. Love soothes the path and shows the way. Sounds simple does it not?

Love is the most powerful energy in the universe and the sharpest sword in God's Army. We need each and every one of the Light Workers on Our Team - Now. Continue working on your "Homework." Use Kuthumi's checklist. Check your progress. Continue your Lord's Prayer Chorus and please use my new meditation. These truly are "short cuts" to your homeward journey to your heavenly home and your retraining to take your place with the Ascended Masters.

As promised, these Lessons are kept brief to give you the maximum time to work on your "homework" to organize your affairs. Make your decisions and complete your business while there is still time. Share your Love. Go about your tasks with peace, joy and harmony in your hearts. Live each day to the fullest, as though it is your last day on earth - it may be. Have Courage and Accept the reality of Ascension.

With these thoughts I will close this Lesson. Call upon Me, Ashtar, members of his Command, or any of the Ascended Masters in the Great White Brotherhood. We are ready to assist you with your "Homework" in any way that is needed.

Love to each and every one of you, My Dear Ones, Sananda

Lesson 16

Greetings, Dear Ones, This is **Archangel Michael**. My message this morning is rather urgent. We are anxious to assist you in your practice of the Ascension process. Using your New Meditation together with your Lord's Prayer choruses, you are becoming much lighter. You are beginning to loosen your earthbound ties. Please call upon me to assist you in this phase of the process. With the assistance of my mighty sword, I will swiftly sever those earthbound ties when you enter your pyramid. Your Merkabah can then descend and enable you to soar throughout the Universe during your meditation. Upon entering your pyramid, declare your desired destination. Start slowly until you feel comfortable with the process. Relax, smile and enjoy yourself. You are embarking upon a great adventure soaring through the Universe using Love Power Energy.

Please call upon me, I love you and want to help you along with your speedy evolution. We are most anxious to receive your help. The need is great and the time is short. We do not wish to pressure you, we want to help you set your priorities.

This process is going to be very pleasant. Winding up your worldly affairs will truly be a lot of fun since you are operating out of Love. Never feel discouraged with your progress. Take one step at a time, repeat the Lord's Prayer and use Sananda's New Meditation. Listen to the telepathic messages being broadcast to you by the Ascended Masters, your Angels, and Members of the Great White Brotherhood. We are at hand to assist you in whatever matters that you feel you cannot easily accomplish or the details and decisions that you labor over. Just call me by name or any of my host of Angels who are watching over you, alert for your call for assistance. My Mighty Sword is available to perform a Psychic Rescue. You are now encircled and protected with my Blue Flame. We have been joyfully anticipating this service to you for many centuries and it will be our pleasure to assist you. Life in the dense body can be somewhat overwhelming. Be assured that your affairs will all fall into place easily and with your full consent and approval.

Be assured that I love you very much and my host of Angels are watching over you always.

Archangel Michael

Lesson 17

Dear Ones, this is **Sananda**. We were happy to attend your impromptu meeting last evening. It is our hope that there will be many such meetings. Wherever you meet, we will be sure to be there. Many members of the Great White Brotherhood are quite anxious to address your group. We, here in the Hierarchy, have anticipated the quickening of Mother Earth for many centuries. We are joyous that the time is at hand. There will be much happiness and an outpouring of love. Do not be afraid. You will find much pleasure in the coming activities. Love God. Love yourself and forgive yourself unconditionally. Then radiate that love to everyone you encounter. We repeat for emphasis. The process is extremely simple.

Love God With All Your Heart
With All Your Mind And With All Your Soul.

Last evening Betty channeled an addition to our New Meditation, (see page 89). I think that you will find this a pleasant addition. It has been designed to assist you with your practice cruise throughout the galaxy. First you will stretch your wings, in your golden pyramid, and take short trips. You will find this medium of travel very relaxing. This is our aim. Take your daily "vacation." First, to the location that we have selected for you. Then as you become more adept at this mode of travel, you may select any destination that you desire. Go there, have a look around, enjoy the sights and sounds. Gain all knowledge, stay as long as you like, and then return at your leisure. You are practicing Ascension.

The time is short. The quickening and necessary cleansing is at hand. We wish that we could give you an exact date. It would greatly assist us in our preparations, as well. You are Our Team. We need your assistance. You are all good soldiers in service to Mankind. Our Army must exercise and tone-up, build your skills. Be ready at a moment's notice. Learn to use your Golden Pyramid. Check it over, maintain it well. Keep it in readiness for an alert call to duty. It is your spaceship, built just for you.

Being responsible human beings, many of you have registered concerns about the effect your ascension will have upon your families. Your Angels will appear to your loved ones and guide them through their processes in settling your affairs. It is our hope that your loved ones work on their readiness and can join you. Your main concern now is to prepare your Ascension Temple. Continue with your Lord's Prayer Chorus. Your light is growing and intensifying daily. It is of great assistance to us, thank you. It is a joy to go about our duties basking in your light and love and the melodious music of your voices. Become thoroughly familiar with our New Meditation and let yourself be led into your meditation with triple choruses of the Lord's Prayer.

I will close this lesson with a reminder to work on your "homework." Come to class prepared to participate. Spread your ever growing store of Love to all you encounter.

My Blessings to you, I Love you very much.

Sananda

Lesson 18

Good Morning, Dear Ones. This is **Kuthumi**. We have been kept very busy in the Universe. We are making every endeavor to avoid as much human suffering as possible during this time of the reconfiguration of Mother Earth. We do look forward to the help of each and every Starseed and Light Worker who is now incarnated on Earth.

This is a call to diligence. Our work is made much easier with your assistance. Let your light shine. We love working in the light of your Love. Your acts of kindness and consideration to one another and with all those you encounter. Your voices raised in the Lord's Prayer and your use of Sananda's New Meditation lights up your corner of the world and shines directly throughout the Universe. We appreciate this surge of Love Energy that we can utilize to telepathically contact more of our Light Workers.

Many new channels have developed throughout the Midwest; in the Heart of the Dove. We are very pleased that many new study groups are forming to work on the Lessons that we are transmitting. Thank you so much, it adds much pleasure to our daily lives as we are going about our tasks. While it is an extremely busy time for the Ascended Masters, I must say that it is a very joyous time. We have been preparing for these changes for a very, very long time. We are looking forward to your return to our ranks. We need your help and we need it now. When the final earth cleansing occurs, many catastrophic earth changes will take place in rapid succession causing a domino effect.

Each and everyone of you will be most grateful for your telepathic abilities when this occurs. You will receive valuable directions that will lead you to a safe place and enable you to lend assistance to those less fortunate Souls who will be filled with fear and panic. You will be able to set up emergency stations to care for the most basic human needs. You will be able to create calm out of chaos.

When the final cleansing occurs, the earth will be completely reconfigured in an instant. Where there were mountains, there will be valleys. Where there were deserts, there will be fresh flowing streams, rivers and lakes. Where there were giant metropolises, only villages will remain. All wars will cease. Hunger will exist everywhere. Huge farms and feed lots will disappear.

All the Souls on earth will be evacuated. Each Soul will be taken to the place where their stage of evolution dictates for the benefit of their continued Soul growth.

This Lesson is not intended to shock you. We merely want to awaken you to the reality of end times - final earth cleansing and evacuation. This Lesson is to help you visualize how much your help will be needed and to realize that the time for your rapid evolution and preparation for Ascension is now. It could be today, it could be tomorrow. Are you ready? Each and every one of you will be needed. You are needed now. You need to choose. Will you choose to Ascend on the first wave? We sincerely hope that you will. Continue your "Homework." Practice Ascension in your Golden Pyramid. Relax and enjoy yourself as you Meditate. Call upon any of us, here in the Great White Brotherhood. We are on hand to help you make your many decisions or to give you strength and wisdom to handle any task. We want to help you clear the way and welcome your return to our ranks for retraining. Really, relax, this is going to be a lot of fun. We do Love each and every one of you.

Good Luck,

Kuthumi

Lesson 19

Dear Ones, This Is **Saint Germain** and I have come to Reinforce all previous Lessons, but, in particular, to ask you to review your beginning Lessons on Unconditional Love and Unconditional Forgiveness. We cannot emphasize this basic lesson too much. Let's start with yourselves, have you truly accomplished unconditional love and forgiveness of yourself? This sounds easy and you think, "Oh sure." But in reality, can you truly say that you have? Every earthbound creature carries around so much guilt. It is cumulative. You collect more and more guilt, life after life, thus creating a very dense body which is tied very firmly to the cycle of reincarnation in an effort to achieve oneness with God.

Diligent application of the Lord's Prayer Choruses and Sananda's new Meditation is designed to loosen your Soul from your dense body. This is our promised "short cut" that will break your cycle of birth and help you take a giant leap in evolution. Daily practice of your Ascension through meditation brings your daily life into focus and you can relax and love yourself. Therefore, building your Love Energy to overflowing where you are compelled to share your love with all you encounter. Reach out and touch someone, as the saying goes - reach out and Love someone, is what we suggest. Feel the thrill when you have made someone happy, have lifted their burden and shared their joy!

We have a rather selfish motive, we want you to rejoin our ranks. We need your help. We are facing a gigantic task and we are calling our Light Workers to report back home - ASAP. Form groups with other Starseeds and Light Workers and meditate together. Build Our Team. Enjoy being together. Get to know one another. Set an example as a loving human being. Put your lives in order, cut your earthbound ties. Prepare for Evacuation and

Ascension. The time of the quickening is at hand. The time to prepare your Ascension Temple is now. This is your Number One Priority.

Love God, My Dear Ones. Love God With All Your Heart, With All Your Mind And With All Your Soul.

If we seem to repeat ourselves when we address you, it is because the solution is so simple that it is mostly overlooked. Love is the answer. When you approach a problem with Love for all concerned, the solution will become manageable. We, of the Hierarchy and the Great White Brotherhood are always available to help you. Just ask, call us by name, do not hesitate. We love you and want to help and know that you will need our assistance to speed your evolution. We know that you are quite capable of handling your own affairs, given enough time. That is where there is a problem. The time is short. The cleansing and quickening of Mother Earth is at hand. Decisive action is needed to wind up your affairs. Our Army is on Call. Your orders could come momentarily. We want you to be ready for that call.

Know that We love each and every one of you very, very much. It has been my pleasure to represent the Brotherhood and to be with you today. Please do not hesitate to call upon me, I am your teacher.

Devotedly, your Servant,

Saint Germain

Lesson 20

Dear Ones, This is **Sananda**. It is my pleasure to greet my dear Starseeds and Light Workers. We enjoy working and communicating with each of you. Your radiance is a sight to behold and your Love Energy grows and glows as proof of your diligence in your "Homework" efforts. Thank you very much for your assistance.

My Lesson today deals with facing your Doubts and Fears. I believe I warned you that Fear and Doubt would surface. Fear and Doubt are the mechanisms that test your Faith and strengthen it when they are overcome.

You now may be feeling that you are a victim of a gigantic hoax. That you are caught up in a fantasy of self aggrandizement or some sort of fraud. You ask, "Why do I suddenly perceive myself as some Ascended Master?" Perhaps at times you feel rather silly. Maybe you have begun to feel that you should chuck it all and get on with your life. Let me assure you that this is a perfectly natural reaction to the pressure that this training has extracted. Your regular routine daily life, as you know it, has been disrupted. You are beginning to wonder if this emphasis on unconditional love and forgiveness of yourself isn't just a matter of rebellion. You ask, "Am I just feeling sorry for myself? Have I just dreamed up all this to bolster my ego?"

Now let me ask you a few questions. Why are millions of people, just like yourself experiencing the same things that you are experiencing at this time in history? Why are you hearing so much about Angels? Why are ordinary people channeling the Masters? Why are millions of people commenting that they are hearing music intruding and rolling in their consciousness? Why are so many people feeling elated and filled with love of their fellow man despite the many horrors and injustices that are happening around the globe?

There is a God in Heaven and Love is the Answer. You perceive yourself as an Ascended Master who has been reincarnated at this End Time, because, you contracted many, many lives ago to help mankind at this time of cataclysmic Earth Changes and cleansing. I confirmed that this was true. You have awakened to the truth. You have been recalled to duty. All you Starseeds and Light Workers have responded to the clarion call. You recognize these truths in your heart of hearts.

Faith in God and yourself is needed now. Have Faith that I Sananda, Ashtar and his Starfleet Crew, Kuthumi, Archangel Michael, Saint Germain and all the Great White Brotherhood love each and every one of you. We need you and look forward to your return home as Ascended Masters who can work along with us in this challenging work that is occurring even as we speak. We look forward to joy and brotherhood as we work together lending assistance in the Three Levels of Ascension and the Final Evacuation at the End Time. Strengthen your Faith and Love God With All Your Heart, With All Your Soul and All Your Mind. We are proud of you.

Continue with your "Homework" - your Lord's Prayer Chorus and practice your Ascension with my New Meditation. Review your earlier Lessons and perform your acts of Love and Devotion to all you encounter in your daily lives. All your Fears and Doubts will soon disappear. Call upon your Angels. Call upon Mary, she has asked me to tell you she is at hand and wants to help in your times of need or uncertainty. All the members of the Great White Brotherhood are at hand waiting for your telepathic messages.

Your faithful servant,

SANANDA

Lesson 21

Dear Ones, Greetings, This is **Saint Germain**. I have planned to stress Togetherness for our Lesson today. We encourage you to work on your own cleansing first and foremost. When you can come together as a group of Light Workers who have accomplished Unconditional Love and Forgiveness of Self, only then can you work in Love and Harmony as a Team of Masters. For you will have mastered yourself. This is no easy task. Love Energy pours easily from a pure heart. Love God, Love Yourself and Love One Another. Sounds easy as - one, two, three!

We know that on the Earth Plane there is much competition for your time and energies. Please know that I am ready, willing and able to assist you in your endeavors and cover you with a mantle of the Purple Flame. You cannot fail in your efforts. Together we can strip away your dense, earthbound body and lift you into your fifth dimensional light body.

There is an urgent need to work together. Time is short. The cleansing and cataclysmic earth changes have begun. Please work on these matters while there is still time. We are now telepathically reaching many of you as evidence of your continuing Meditation and Lord's Prayer Chorus. Your Auric Light is beautiful to behold, the Music is magnificent, and together they create a Love Energy Cable to the Universe that is static free. The environment of Love and Light that you have created for us is of great benefit in our earthward communication efforts.

Your continued diligence and sincere efforts in spreading the Love and Joy that emanates from your own newfound Self Love and Forgiveness is spreading a new awareness of God's Love to all you encounter. This creates the desire in those you encounter to emulate the Radiant Love that you project. God's Love is being spread in ever widening circles in a pyramid fashion radiating in ever broadening areas. There are millions of Light Workers throughout the earth that are now intensively working on their own spirituality. This is our Army, working on their own Ascension Temples and battling negativity.

All Starseeds and Light Workers working together eradicating negativity in all corners of the earth can eliminate the necessity of much of the cataclysmic earth changes and can save many souls through the earth plane.

Ponder on these truths. Renew your efforts in Unconditional Love and Forgiveness of Self. That is the giant step. Overcome your self doubts and fears. They are your greatest enemy to your evolution and attainment of Unconditional Self Love and Forgiveness.

Wherever possible, get together to practice our New Meditation lifting yourself into your Golden Pyramid and take a trip to your secret Island to ground your emotional body. When you enter your Golden Pyramid, you activate your Fifth Dimensional Body and your Eighth Chakra. Call down your Merkabah and fill your Pyramid with the Golden White Light that filters down from the top and flows around the interior and exterior of your pyramid. This is your Spaceship. Carefully inspect your ship and keep it in top working order in readiness for your call to active duty. You are our Army and are on alert. Maintain your training exercises and do your "Homework" so you will be prepared when you are called.

It has been my pleasure to address you today. I love you very much.

Saint Germain

Lesson 22

Good Morning, Betty, This is **Kuthumi**. Welcome back. We have been very, very busy in the Universe. As you know there has been a major Quake in Japan. We avoided great loss of life since the epicenter was deep under the Ocean Floor. Japan is a very vulnerable area.

As you see, Dear Ones, the cleansing is in full swing. We have been working diligently trying to shield earth inhabitants and save lives. Your building Love Power has been of considerable assistance. As has the cooperative efforts of all our Light Workers throughout the earth plane. Yes, there is growing awareness all over the planet. For this we are gratified. We admonish you to continue your Prayer and Meditations; it is generating more power than you can ever imagine and is vital to our efforts to save mankind on earth.

Project Earth Ascension is a challenging, but not impossible, task. It is a unique experiment in the long history of the Galaxy. There have been planets throughout the Galaxy over eons of time who have destroyed themselves through greed and lust for power. Through wars and destruction of their environments and utter disregard for the lives of the humanity populating those planets.

Sananda, Members of the Hierarchy and the Great White Brotherhood, the Archangels and all the Ascended Masters deemed it an abomination that the beautiful Mother Earth be sacrificed through the actions of Greed and Hatred. Project Earth Ascension was borne and has been in the planning stages for over two thousand years. Your return and incarnation into your present earthbound body is all part of the plan. As difficult as we realize it is for you to do, you must now shed your dense body and prepare to return to active duty. You are our Team and our Army. You have populated Planet Earth and lived many lives in your dense body. You are commanded to get in shape, shed your dense body, and prepare to take your rightful place as an Ascended Master. Time is short. You must use it wisely if you are to be ready for Ascension. We have noticed some "backsliding" due to your Fears and Doubts. You are our beloved brothers and sisters. You have been as asleep and have taken root on the earth plane.

Call upon Archangel Michael to assist you in cutting your earthbound ties and cover you with his Blue Flame. Call upon your Angels to help you set your priorities and help you keep your momentum that you have been building with your prayers and meditations. Practice your Ascension in your Golden Pyramid. Wear it on the Eighth Chakra. Ask Saint Germain to cover you in his PURPLE FLAME and travel to the places of your choice throughout the earth plane and any destination in the Universe. This is your heritage. Practice, practice, practice and be ready. Maintain your Golden Pyramid and your Merkabah. This is your Spaceship. Be Ready. You Are On Alert. We Need You At our Side!

We love you very much.

Your Faithful Servant,

Kuthumi

Lesson 23

Dear One, this is **Saint Germain**. I have a message to impart this morning. Time is short and there is still much to do to prepare for the End Days. Shall we begin.

Dear Ones, Again, it is always such a pleasure to greet you and visit with you. It would be our pleasure to come, visit and converse with you. As it is, we must rely upon the written word and your willingness to read and absorb our words of wisdom. Today, I would like you to ponder further on the preparations for your Ascension.

It is our observation that most of our awakened Starseeds and Light Workers are eagerly awaiting the opportunity to Ascend. However, we do detect some lingering Fear in your hearts. Fear of leaving the known for the unknown. Fear of living and fear of dying. Fear of rejection at the moment of Ascension.

My Dear Ones, you must put your Fear behind you and have Faith. You cannot Ascend when there is Fear in your heart. You cannot leave your dense body so long as fear occupies your Heart, your Mind or your Body. Replace your Fear with Love. When you truly love and forgive yourself unconditionally, only then can you begin to conquer your Fear.

You are now covered in my Purple Flame. Nothing can harm you except your own Fears. Call upon me for help. I am here for you. Call upon your Angels as instructed by Archangel Michael and ask to be covered by his Blue Flame and be freed from your Earthbound Ties with his Magic Sword. We love you very, very much and need you Now.

Continue to practice Ascension through your Prayers and Meditation. Travel wherever you like and stay as long as you like while in your Golden Pyramid which you have fueled with your acts of Loving Kindness and Unconditional Self Love. Examine your collections of crystals that we have provided for your use. Rearrange them to suit your own designs. Relax and ground your emotional body. Walk along our fine crystal beaches and refresh yourself in the pure pristine water. Take your dependent animals along for companionship or call upon any member of the Great White Brotherhood and we will be at your side.

Love Is The Answer. Love God With All Your Mind, with All Your Heart and with All Your Soul. Love Yourself Unconditionally and Forgive Yourself Unconditionally. Share Your Love With All You Encounter.

Your Faithful Servant
Saint Germain

Lesson 24

Dear Ones, Starseeds, Light Workers, All - It Is My Pleasure To Greet You And Bring My Blessings To You This Morning. Mother Mary Is Here Too And Sends Her Blessings To You. We Appreciate the diligent work that you have all been doing. We appreciate your raising your voices in the Lord's Prayer and your Ascension practice with my New Meditation.

We realize that my Meditation is somewhat difficult for many of you to use since it requires you to exhale much deeper than many other meditations require. More frequent and deeper exhalation was designed into this meditation to release more of your fears and accumulated negativity, and to expand your lung capacity and bring in more joy, love and happiness with each inhalation. Daily use of this meditation will accelerate your evolution and release your light body from your dense body. And, expand your LOVE ENERGY to light our telepathic path and better communicate with each of you.

Practice, practice, practice. You are My Team. Be ready for an instant alert. Use your pyramid often. Enjoy frequent excursions throughout the Universe. Call upon me. Call upon Ashtar. Call upon Archangel Michael and his Angels. Call upon Saint Germain. We all delight in taking an instant vacation to pleasant places. We want to help with all your concerns. We don't issue advice unless called upon to do so.

Smile, be happy and love yourself - we do. Love God and spread that love to all you encounter. Be a beacon of God's Love and Light.

Blessings to you all from Mary and I.

Sananda

PART V

Saint Germain's Channeled lecture on Grounding your emotional body and answers member questions.

SAINT GERMAIN CHANNELED BY BETTY HUDSON

Mission, Kansas

You have no idea how beautiful you are. You glow and your auras are such beautiful, beautiful colors. Streams of light in all shades of reds, pinks and blues. These are your colors and those you are familiar working with. A tremendous white light is shed from each and every one of you. And, it is a tremendous help to all of us. It helps us come through to you.

I just want to talk for a few minutes today about Grounding Your Emotional Bodies. This can be done with service to others. This is a different concept than you think of as service. This does not mean that you are a servant to others. This you might say was true, but it is service to yourself, it is service to mankind. The most important way of providing service is to first prepare your own bodies, your own intellects, your own emotional bodies. You have carried such a burden of emotions. You are all so sensitive that when you harm someone else by your thoughts or deeds, you carry a great package of guilt. You must now learn to release that guilt. This is what you are working through.

You may find that you are having physical pain due to this guilt. This has created stress and all manner of physical ills to your dense body.

If you cannot hear my transmission, please so indicate. I believe that I can turn up the volume.

As far as the children are concerned, little children will go with their parent who ascends. The parent that normally has the care of that dependent child or children, as the case may be. Or, the one whose responsibility it is to care for these children.

They will be self sufficient. Your children are Starseeds. They are just being called home sooner than you have been called forward.

There will be three waves of Ascension. It is our hope that all of you will prepare now for the First Ascension. Do not be dis-

couraged because it has sometimes been characterized as being "childlike." That we will accept those for the First Ascension who are "childlike." That reference is that your Faith is like a child. A young child has faith in its parents. We want you to show your Faith in us and in the process. We think as you are going through these Lessons you are growing. Using the checklist you have monitored your own progress and you will see how you are growing in the Light. You will have confirmation through your increased telepathic abilities. You will be feeling lighter and, yes, younger as you progress and as you use Sananda's Meditation which was carefully engineered by all of us here in the Hierarchy and the great White Brotherhood. This has been mathematically calculated to match the goal of Ascension to the Universe. The entire Meditation. The color schemes, the crystals, the use of the crystals, the chakras, the movement upward through the chakras, and the creation of your pyramid. This is your creation through visualization. And, you are creating a station for your Merkabah.

All of us in the Great White Brotherhood and the Hierarchy took many, many lifetimes on Earth to Ascend into the Universe and hold our present position as Masters. You are being honored to have a much shorter time. These Lessons and this Meditation are what you call "short cuts." We would have enjoyed having "short cuts." The important thing for you to remember is Love. Love Yourself and Forgive Yourself and share that Love with all you encounter.

We must let Betty come back - she is getting restless. It has been my pleasure to address you today. I love you all.

I AM - Saint Germain

* * * * *

PART VI

Sananda's New Meditation Channeled and expanded at Lake Waukomis, Mo.

Sananda's New Meditation Channeled By Betty Hudson

Lake Waukomis, MO.

Take a deep breath, hold it - release it slowly.

Bring yourself down slowly, down, down, down
- deeper, deeper, deeper.

Release it slowly, slowly, slowly going down,
- deeper, deeper, deeper.

If this Meditation puts you in a Channeling state, it will be quite acceptable and we'll be happy to hear what your channel has to say.

Breathe in positive energy. Breathe in love, light, joy and happiness. Exhale all that is negative - all that is burdensome. Let the joy and happiness come through. We love each of you.

Once more take a deep breath - hold it and let it out slowly, down, down, down - deeper, deeper, deeper. See the columns of crystals. Clear white crystals. Fields and fields of smooth, clear white crystals of all sizes and shapes. Reach for them, feel them, hold them in your hands. Meditate on these clear white crystals. See your pathway clear. See yourself in this light, surrounded by these clear white crystals.

Breathe in another deep breath, deeper, deeper, deeper - hold it. Exhale. Feel yourself going down, down, down. See the beautiful bright golden yellow crystals. Feel the crystals. Enjoy the crystals. Step on the crystals, they are small enough and smooth. Feel the energy entering your body. Meditate on the pure golden light.

Inhale deeply. Feel yourself rising higher, higher and higher. Hold it. Exhale, down, down, down - deeper, deeper, and deeper. See the beautiful blue crystals - clear light blue crystals - light blue as the sky. Sit by the water. Put your feet in the water and feel the smooth, clear, light blue stones. Let the water cool you and soothe you. Meditate by the water and feel the love, feel the energy force entering your chakras one by one.

Inhale - deeper, deeper and deeper. Hold your breath. Exhale. Going down, down, down. See the beautiful clouds and mist. See the fields of rose quartz through the clearing mist and clouds. Sort through them carefully. Selecting just the crystals that seem right for you. Pick up two hands full and bring them to your heart chakra. This is the love crystal. This is what you are reaching for - Love, Love, Love, Love. Inhale. Bring in more and more of this love energy. Bring it up and up - hold it, enjoy it. Release this energy slowly and bring it down, down, down.

Inhale. We are going to your throat chakra. See the fields of beautiful green crystals of many shades and hues. There are many, many crystals scattered around. Run your hands over the crystals. Choose as many as you wish. These crystals have been placed here for you to use. Now find the biggest one you can find and place it on your throat chakra. Feel the vibrations rising throughout your body. You now can express your love to all you encounter. Express your love to all creatures big and small who deserve your love. Everyone does.

Inhale. Bring in more and more breath. You are going to need this to express your love. Exhale - down, down, down - deeper, deeper, deeper. Bring in the bright blue light of the Lapis Lazuli. See them scattered all around you. Feel the different sizes and shapes. Choose just the right shape, size and density. Bring them up to your Third Eye Chakra. Enjoy it. See the pictures. Feel the strength and energy of the Lapis Lazuli opening this very vital chakra. Take a deep breath. Feel yourself rising up, up, up. Hold your breath as long as you can and enjoy this beautiful feeling. Stay as long as you wish. You will find yourself hearing and receiving all knowledge. Now release your breath and come down, down, down.

Inhale. Take another deep breath reaching higher and higher. Here we are, back to clear white crystals. These are much bigger, much brighter, and much harder in density. Find just the perfect stone for you. Hold it in both hands. Feel its intense energy. Place it on your crown chakra. Now take as many of these sparkling, clear crystals as you desire and create a crown. Wear your crown well. Feel the Love Energy. This is the Christ, God Energy. Enjoy it. You deserve it. You will want to share it with all you encounter. Exhale and come down. Now take a deep breath and return to the crown chakra. Dare to think higher. Visualize a golden pyramid of your own creation constructed of blocks of pure gold. It is made just for you. Create a door just large enough for you to crawl through and to bring in your dependent pets, if you wish. Upon entering this pyramid, you are moving into your multi-dimensional body. Feel how you are lifting yourself up. You are practicing lifting yourself above your earthbound ties. Stay as long as you like.

Now you are going on vacation. We're going on a trip, stay in your Golden Pyramid. We are all going together, keep lifting higher and higher and higher. See the light coming down through to top of your pyramid surrounding you. If you want, call upon myself, Sananda, call upon Ashtar, call upon St. Michael, call upon Saint Germain, call upon your Angels, any of the members of the Great White Brotherhood. There will be room to put us in your Golden Pyramid. We are going to have fun. This is a vacation.

We are going to a beautiful South Seas Island. You have your crystals with you, you are wearing your crown. Let's go to the Island. We have arrived. Open the door of your Golden Pyramid and step out right at the edge of the water. Take your shoes off, step into the water. See the beautiful smooth, shiny, black stones. Sit down in the water and ground yourself. Stay as long as you like. You are grounded on this beautiful island. You can now release your emotional body and come to oneness. Stay as long as you like and walk along the beach. There are all manner of other crystals. Garnets, emeralds and many other crystals of your choice, find your favorites. Take as many as you like. You can stay as long as you like. Stay until you feel refreshed.

Now we will return. Remember that you have lifted off the earth plane. You have traveled. When you are ready, go back to your pyramid, open the door, crawl in, sit in your very comfortable chair. Prepare to return, it only takes an instant. While we are still above the earth, call upon Archangel Michael to use his magic sword and swiftly cut below your feet to loosen your ties, your earthbound ties. You can now return home of your own free will and feel refreshed.

Now we need to let Betty come back. It has been such a pleasure to be with you.

Goodnight.

This is SANANDA

* * * * *

PART VII

JODI BOTTIGER'S

Blue Springs Discovery Class Channelings

Sananda introduces Saint Germain

Sananda introduces Archangel Michael and Mother Mary.

Discovery Class Channelings

Rewards received following the ascension path are many and varied. Paramount on my list of blessings are the many beautiful Souls who have touched my life since transmission of The Lessons began.

I have encountered hundreds of loving Souls in my journey towards Oneness. Listing each and every one is not possible at this writing. This alone could be another book.

Significant among them is one shining example in Blue Springs, Missouri...Jodi Bottiger. Jodi is clairvoyant, clairaudient and clairscentient, a Reiki Master and a Hypnotherapist. Her eighth chakra is fully functional as attested by her communications with the Masters when planning her classes for the Discovery Group. Incidentally, the first day I attended her class, The Masters suggested "Channeling" as a topic for the class.

My dear friends and Family of Light workers, Dennis Hockett and Gini Newcomb, were members of Jodi's class and I felt compelled to join them. Reluctant to seem competitive with the lessons that Jodi was offering and very thrilled to participate in her inspired classes I did not mention what I had been receiving from the Masters. As classes progressed, I revealed to Jodi what I had been receiving in automatic writing and trance channeling the Masters. She was pleased and asked me to channel for the class. Sananda, Saint Germain, Archangel Michael and Mother Mary were anxious to address the group as taped and transcribed .

BETTY HUDSON CHANNELS SANANDA & SAINT GERMAIN *for the Discovery Study Group*

12/07/94 8:00 pm

Good Evening, this is **Sananda**. *I have an honored guest for you tonight that would like to address you. Saint Germain is here. He chuckled over your violent flame. He too thought it was violent, but that is quite all right. I just came to greet you and introduce Saint Germain. To give my blessings and I will say good night. Saint Germain is anxious to talk to you.*

Saint Germain began,

We have been very busy all over the galaxy. There have been many, many things for us to do. But we have had much help. There are loving beings throughout the galaxy. They look like you and I and they love you, as I love you, as Sananda loves you.

My message tonight is that I want you to have courage. This is not always easy. Courage will erase doubt and fear and will be replaced with love. Your most important mission is to love yourself and forgive yourself unconditionally. Many of you think, particularly our young ones, "I don't have anything to forgive". But any negative thoughts over the centuries over many, many lifetimes have added to your dense body. And we want to help you to release yourself, - I repeat, to release yourself - from your dense body. No one can do that for you. This is your job and we are here to help.

Do I have a question?

Saint Germain, the ceremony coming up, 12:12, is there anything specific that you would suggest that we do?

12:12 is an important event. The most important event in all of your lives. The most important for many thousands of earth years. It is the gateway to immortality. Your figure eight, as you describe it, is the symbol for immortality. It shows how we can cross over and you can cross over. Did I answer your question?

Is there something specific we can physically do to help with this?

Your prayers and meditations, your attitude, your intent. Your intent is most important. Your thoughts. You will have noticed and will be noticing the quickening of time. There is very little time left. Be most aware of your thoughts. Do not spend time in idle speculation. You may get something you do not want. So be most careful what you ask for. It will manifest quickly. May I have another question?

Has the first ascension taken place?

There was an ascension some 10, 12, 13 years ago. That was not the three waves we refer to at this time. That event was completed. That was in preparation for what is happening now. We are so, so, looking forward to all or you joining us and regaining what is rightfully yours. Earth ascension was an experiment. It is an experiment under the leadership of Sananda, who 2,000 years ago was known as Jesus. The earth has had many cleansings. There have been many cleansings of various planets in the galaxies they simply blew up. Our experiment, we dearly love our beloved mother earth, she is our prize, our experiment was planned as an experiment. If we ask ascended masters to return to earth to enter the dense body lifetime after lifetime and then live and breathe as earth creatures, then at the time of cleansing we would have our starseeds together. That would give us assistance in helping all those souls who have not had this opportunity. It is an opportunity for everyone who is now seeking to accelerate their evolution.

We as Masters, did not have this privilege. We worked many, many, many lifetime to overcome our greed and selfish desires and puri fy our love of self so that we may sit at the right hand of God. This is now the opportunity that you are offered. We are somewhat, well more than somewhat, disappointed that our starseeds did not retain more of their ascended master skills. These skills are not easily attained. But there are many who are now channeling who have telepathic abilities. This is created through love. It gives us clear passage to reach you. We must come down in vibrations and you must come up in vibrations. Obviously tonight there are good vibrations in this room. We love you all and look forward to your joining us. We have had many ask us what date this will all occur. Your 12:12 is a significant gateway. It is not the first wave. We do not know the date of the first wave. Only God knows.

Saint Germain, if you would, send a beam of healing energy into Betty. Her energy field is starting to draw in. If you would re-energize her. (pause) Thank you.

She is fine now.

Saint Germain, I have been sharing these lessons with my family. Should I urge them to participate with me?

Whatever you do in love is helpful to them. But ask them if they want you to do that. You cannot bring someone along. You must do this for yourself and they must do it for themselves. More ques tions? No? Then I will say goodnight.

Our thanks to you Saint Germain and to Betty for these gifts of pure truth for our group.

BETTY HUDSON CHANNELS SANANDA, ARCHANGEL MICHAEL & MOTHER MARY
for the Discovery Study Group

12/14/94

Good evening, this is **Sananda**. *I have an honored quest who would like to address your Discovery Study Group this evening. He has charge over a multitude of angels.*

You know him as **Saint Michael**..

Good evening, Dear Ones. It is a pleasure to be with you all. I have wanted to address your group for some time now. Many of my angels are here. I have my mighty sword to assist you and my blue flame to bless you and cover you with a mantle of protection.

There was much discussion in your group tonight about fear and courage. God is Love. Fear is the opposite of Love. You have no reason to fear. When you grow in acceptance and digest this information. Fear is erased by faith. Have faith in yourself and your capabilities. You made a contract many many years ago to be here at this time. You volunteered to be of assistance in the last days. You are all highly evolved souls, you just have poor memories. But that is understandable.

You are given the opportunity to evolve very, very quickly and this must be so. You are much needed in our army. Yes, I am a military man. There is much need for rearming yourselves in the light, truth and love of God. This is your shield and buckler. You must learn to loosen your dense bodies and I am here to help you. Just call upon me and I will help you with my mighty sword, as you loosen your bonds, your earth bound bonds, I sever those. Never fear, my aim is good. No harm will come to you. You are on the most exciting journey. We are anticipating your joining us. We have been together before and we want you to come home and be with us.

I heard concern about your families, about your children, about your husband or your wife. I will send my angels to inform them when you ascend. Your main purpose for learning a new meditation is to prepare yourself for ascension. It is a practice in ascensionion. The more you practice now, the sooner you will learn your true history. You will have a choice at the time of ascension. You do not have to go in the first wave. We hope that you will, you are much needed. You are much needed to participate in re-training as soon as possible. At that time you will have another choice. You may return from your place of origin, if you so desire, or you may stand with us and return to earth and help those who are left behind.

I know you may have many questions. Some questions, I may not answer. You have free will. The earth is the only planet in the universe where you have free will. You have to learn to exercise your free will and to make choices. This is why we stress that you have a choice in what you do. You will not be judged either right or wrong, that is up to you to decide. We love you. You have no idea how much we love you. You are all so beautiful to us. Do I have a question?

Saint Michael, are you also referred to as Archangel Michael?

Yes, indeed.

I'd like to know what talents or gifts that St.Germain said last week that we had forgotten as ascended beings.

I'm not sure what St. Germain said. Would you repeat that?

Those of us who have already ascended and have come back and have forgotten what we could do - before.. (master skills)

This is not something that is a simple answer that I can give now. You will receive this information when you ascend and are retrained in the school there. You will have full knowledge of your real true self. Full soul memory. Does that answer your question? Good. Is there another question?

My 11 year old son would like to know the name of his guardian angel.

Your son actually has three guardian angels. There are times he has more. He is a very special boy. His main angel is Raphael. He has another angel, a very beautiful angel, with the name of Lily. And then, of course, there is Mary. There are many others who come to him. If he desires to know their name, tell him to ask. Is there another question?

I have one. When we ascend, will we actually take our body and leave or will there be anything left of us here on earth?

You will take your body with you. There will be no shell here. When you ascend, you will ascend in an enlightened body. This is why we instruct you to meditate, meditate, meditate, practice, practice, practice. Your meditation is your vehicle, it is your spaceship, particularly your pyramid. Practice often, go on many trips. Feel at home in your pyramid. When you do this as often as possible, your ascension will not be as abrupt. Your retraining will seem instantaneous. You then will have the power to return and assist those you love and you may reclothe yourself in your present body, so you will be recognized and there will seem as though there is no change. If this has been your choice. Remember what I said, you have a choice. When you find out your origin, which may be anywhere in the galaxy, you may want to go home. You may find your twin flame in your training class or waiting for you. You may not want to come home here on Earth. We hope that you will, we need your help and the dear souls here on the Earth plane need your help. You will be informed, telepathically what to do and how to do it.

Those who leave a spouse who has not been following the light, when they see you ascend and are informed by one of our angels, you need not have concern. They will get your message. This is why we have three waves of ascension. We hope all inhabitants of the earth plane will become Christed. No one will occupy the restructured earth by Christed souls. The others will be removed to where they need to be. Do I have another question?

Could the experience I had last night have been avoided or was it something that was sent to me to open me to a higher vibration?

You have correctly assessed the situation. You were given this experience to open and you have processed through this. I love you very much. You are doing a wonderful job. Just call upon me when you want me to cover you with my blue flame and cut your earth bound ties.

Lord Michael, how did Monday's 12:12 energies work out?

We are very glowingly happy at the anchoring of these energies. I'm sure you are feeling this new and heightened energy. This is so much better for us to work with.

Saint Michael, a couple of weeks ago you came to me in my meditation and you gave me my own sword and told me to go get them and I was wondering how I could go get them in the best way for my highest path.

Keep up the good work. We love you, you are our warrior. You are doing a wonderful job. Keep doing the meditation, you will have your inner guidance. I just need to affirm to you that what you are doing. You are on the right path. You need to do this for yourself. We love you.

Saint Michael, I have a tendency to not believe in myself in what I am hearing and what I am feeling and I want to know if I'm on the right path and if the message I am writing and I feel I need to get out to people through my writing is the message that is coming from you all?

Oh yes it is. You are our dear one. We are happy to be writing through you. Please do not stop.

At this time Betty chokes and comes out of Meditation. We give her some time and she is told that Mother Mary wants to come through.

This is **Sananda**, *I want you to know that Mary wants to address your group. I now turn this over to* **Mother Mary.**

Good evening, this is Mary. *I'm so happy you are all here tonight. This has been a wonderful gathering in this joyful season. You are all glowing so well. You give us a wonderful conduit to address you. There is so much peace and harmony in this group. I want to congratulate you on this. We love you dearly. Go out and spread your love. Do not misunderstand me, we do not ask you to evangelize, just by loving yourself and sharing your love with others, this is how they will know that you are someone special and they will want whatever it is that you have. This inner glow, this inner love, they will want the peace and harmony that you exude and they will want to follow the path. I must say good night, I think that Betty has extended enough energy for now. Just remember that we love you all. Goodnight. Mary*

The leader of the group extended thanks to Betty and the Ascended Masters for their gifts of the pure truth to the group.

* * * * *

PART VIII

*** Marina Del Rey, California Letters**

SANANDA

URIEL

SANANDA

Mary and Saint John

December 20, 1994 Marina del Rey, California

Dear One, this is **Sananda**. Greetings and Blessings to you in California. There is a message I wish to impart to all Light Workers and Starseeds.

Dear Ones, Love is the answer. Simply Love. First, Love Yourself unconditionally and Forgive Yourself unconditionally. This message cannot be repeated too often. It is of the utmost importance. Love has great Power to transform Planet Earth. You need not suffer further earthquake destruction. Utilize your God given gift of Love Power to transmute the destructive power of negativity, greed and selfish desire.

Love God with all your heart, with all your mind and with all your Soul. Let love start with you and share it with all you encounter. Spread the power of Love with a simple smile of encouragement. It is infectious. It will spread to all you encounter.

Fear must be replaced by Faith. Time is so short before the End Times. Be of great courage, My Dear Ones. Now is the time to prepare for the coming events. California can be saved from destruction when hearts are linked to hearts across the State. I have dictated a series of lessons to this Scribe and she will share them with you.

I love you all!

Sananda

December 31, 1994 Marina del Rey, California

Dear One, Good Morning, this is **Sananda**. I have a message and my Blessings to impart while you are in California.

Dear Ones, Light Workers and Starseeds. Let me congratulate you on your growing awareness and your expressions of love. Many of you are channeling and spreading your love to all you encounter. Living your self love and becoming fine examples of "love in action."

Love Power is the most powerful energy in the Universe. God is Love. We appreciate the glowing powerful beacon that you become for all the Universe when you operate out of self love. You create a bridge of Light which is a static free communications link with the entire Universe including all of the outer Galaxies.

Love Power provides protection and guidance through telepathic abilities for My Dear Light Workers and Starseeds. Time is short; the cleansing and restructuring of Mother Earth is in progress. You are a vital link in the gridworks and ley lines.

I love you all,

Sananda

January 13, 1995 Marina del Rey, California

Dear One, this is **Uriel**. What a pleasure to greet you! I send you my love and Blessings. You are never alone, Betty. We are always standing by ready to assist when needed. We love you and yours. You have had many trials in your earthbound journey and have learned many lessons along the way. You have shown much courage and devotion to your Master, Our Lord Jesus Sananda.

We are all grateful that you are willing to accept our words and broadcast them to the hearts and minds who are willing to listen.

I am sure that you have met many Light Workers here on the West Coast. There is still much work to do and so little time to spread the word. Just continue to be an example of our love and kindness to all you meet.

Please call upon your Angels, we are standing by with help in the smallest and most difficult tasks. Whatever you need, we want to help you. Do not hesitate. We love you. You've had a big day, relax and refresh yourself through a good night's sleep.

Love,

Uriel, the Archangel

UNCONDITIONAL LOVE

February 6, 1995 4:30 AM Marina del Rey, California

Dear One, this is **Sananda**. I have an important message to impart to be included in our book.

Dear Ones, Greetings to all Light Workers and Starseeds. This is a very important message directed to you regarding the End Time. Mother Earth is being very carefully reconfigured at this time. We are working diligently endeavoring to save as many lives as possible.

We deeply regret the recent earthquake in Kobe, Japan and the huge loss of life. Regrettably shabby construction of many of the buildings was the major cause of the great losses. It is not my place to fix blame.

Unconditional love and unconditional forgiveness is more necessary now. Please do not wait until tomorrow to put this program into practice. Love God. Love yourself, too. Share that love with all you encounter. Work together in love and harmony. Perfect love is not judgmental. Be at peace in your own heart. Concentrate on Self and release all negativity. Forgive yourself for all present and past transgressions through prayer and meditation.

It is my hope that you will choose to participate in this course of enlightenment. It has been designed for you and your conscious efforts toward your self spiritual path and evolution.

I love you all. You are my Dear Ones.
Sananda

June 3, 1995 5:00 AM
Marina del Rey, California

Dear One, this is **Sananda**. We are anxious to resume our daily sessions. It is now timely to complete the book. Do not be concerned about format. That will all be arranged. We do not want you to get mired down in details or worry about equipment. We love you and these are minor details.

Dear Ones, with the anchoring of the new Universal Energies we have a much more open channel to relay our messages to our Light Workers and Starseeds. There are many, many new groups forming throughout the Universe. Many Celestial volunteers have taken on the garment of an earth-dense body and are walking and working among you. Love is the answer. Love will bring peace and harmony where there has been discontent and dissension. Love and forgiveness is the divine answer. Concentrated thoughts of love directed to the Leaders of Earth's trouble spots can relieve much pain and suffering. Love will make the difference. Halt nuclear testing in China!

Love and Blessings, Sananda

UNCONDITIONAL LOVE

June 5, 1995 5:00 AM
Marina del Rey, California

Dear One. This is **Sananda**. We love you and send our Blessings to you this fine morning. Shall we begin.

Dear Ones, Light Workers, All. Now is the time to diligently prepare. Many have made tremendous strides in accomplishing their goals toward Oneness. Enjoying the pleasure of a job well done and the happiness of achievement - the joy of sharing love. Love is not always easy to share. For in the giving of love there is an expectation of gratitude when love is given to an individual. That is where the unconditional love must be expressed. Love must be given without expectation of a Thank You in return.

Love yourself unconditionally. That is the most difficult task. Most reasonably happy Souls feel that they do love them selves unconditionally until one really becomes introspective and that self love is tested. Sometimes tested to the extreme.

Doubts and fears enter into the picture to destroy that contentment with one's self image - one's self esteem. That expression is much bandied about these days by Psychologist - both the professional and the armchair type. Just remember, God is Love. Be still and know that I am God. So says our Father, Lord God Almighty.

Make time to enter your Temple and seek the stillness. Listen to God within your heart. Love will follow and flow with abundance. All your needs will be met. There you will find rich treasures of your Soul. There you will find wholeness and Oneness.

Ponder these things and add them to your store of unconditional love. Accept the love streams that follow. Relearn to love. Relearn forgiveness. That is the path you must follow. We are here with you awaiting your call for assistance. Smile and lift the burden from your brow. See the Light - become the Light. We surround you with Light and Love.. SANANDA

Dear One, this is **John**.

You are very loving and part of God's love. Let your light so shine that all you encounter will be warmed by your radiance. Have courage and have no fear. We are at your beckon call. Your Angels are at your side always and await your call for assistance in any circumstance big or small. We love you very much.

Mary is here with me and wants a few words with you this morning.

Betty, good morning, my dear. There is much positive activity here in the City of Angels. We have many Souls who are now actively functioning in their light bodies. These people will now be coming into your vibration. Meditate and continue your prayers. Do not be discouraged. You feel a sense of urgency and feel that you are not accomplishing your goals. We are well satisfied. You are operating out of unconditional love. We know that it is not always easy to forgive and forget. Have faith and lean on us when the going gets tough. Love God and love yourself for God is love and abides in your heart chakra.

The Lessons that we want to impart are simple and sweet. Love God by loving yourself. All else will follow. Have faith in God and know that you are a part of God. Would he want less for his children? No, no, Dear Ones.

Ask and it shall be given unto you.
Knock and the Gates will be opened.
For yours is the Kingdom of Heaven.

Remember who you are for your journey has been far. You have had many and varied experiences in your earth embodiments. Now is the time to shed your accumulated dense body and let your light shine through.

We love you and send our blessings to you and your loved ones.

Mary and John

EPILOGUE ...

MY VISIONS

Intergalactic Federation Council Conference

Evacuation and Ascension

LIGHT WORKERS CHANNELING

Sylvia Hughey's Poetry - Birth of Divinity

Channeled Reading by Reverend Fern Moreland

Fern Moreland Channels Great White Feather

"MY VISIONS"

INTERGALACTIC FEDERATION COUNCIL CONFERENCE

Since attending the Family of Light Network Organizational Weekend in Wells, Kansas I have had several very vivid visions. It is quite easy to distinguish these visions from dreams. The impact upon my consciousness is undeniable. Months or even years later I can relate these visions in minute detail. Just as if I had really witnessed the event, perhaps even better. I'm not a Trekkie. Rarely do I sit through an entire viewing of one segment of the Star Trek series. However, in my communication with the Ascended masters, I have been advised that millions of volunteers from all over the Universe have assembled to help in the Transformation and Re-birthing of Planet Earth. A giant, benevolent rescue operation is taking place.

It seems that Planet Earth is considered the "Harvard" of the Universe and all the inhabitants are very special souls of Love and it's application in the order of the Universe.

The Dove hovers over Kansas City and the four midwestern states. The wings of the Dove spread from coast to coast. Further, the Dove has been in this position for a very long time and is stationed there to protect the inhabitants of this planet. The ship is invisible to us simply because it exists in a higher dimension and operates on a much higher vibrational frequency.

But I'm getting ahead of myself again. Prior to receiving the detailed information about the Dove, I had a very, very vivid vision where I was attending an important lecture aboard a very large ship. The lecture, or school of instruction, was being presented in a huge, round auditorium that was really more like a stadium. Yet it definitely was not conducted in a stadium. We were in a room of great beauty. The light in the room was luminous and enthralling beyond description. There was a round platform, complete with a lectern, in the center of this auditorium. The platform was encircled with a row of very comfortable, high-backed armchairs. They were occupied by very stately Elders who were dressed in beautiful white robes. There was a stunningly bright, radiant, crystalline glow surrounding these dignitaries. Both male and female elders were represented and seated in this place of honor. I felt highly privileged to be witnessing the meeting in this wondrous place.

There was a hush in the auditorium as the lecture began. I now know that our speaker was Sananda. He was very tall, stately and dignified in his demeanor. He had long dark blonde shoulder length curly hair that he had brushed back behind his ears. His eyes were blue and most exceptional. They seemed to broadcast love and affection to each individual in the audience. He strode across the platform and seemed to be personally addressing each of us.

I had paper and pen in hand and kept feverishly reminding myself that I must remember every word of the lecture to take back home and share this urgent message. There was no sound in the auditorium, save the sound of the Master's voice.

All of a sudden, out of nowhere, it seemed, a messenger of powerful Viking proportions attired in a space uniform appeared on the platform. He politely saluted Sananda saying, "I am Centaur. I have an urgent message for you." Sananda returned his salute and stepped aside, apologizing to the audience. After a brief discussion with the messenger, Centaur, he turn again to the audience and said, "You must forgive me, I am urgently needed elsewhere."

Then an odd thing happened. Centaur went to work with what appeared to be an extremely hefty ratchet-type wrench, about the size of a canoe paddle, in an effort to loosen and open a huge boulder that was now on the stage. As he proceeded to loosen this boulder, a bright white light was emitted that grew in brilliance and intensity as the boulder was loosened. Sananda stepped into this light and ascended in a flash like a reverse comet and disappeared into the stratosphere.

I have since theorized that this was a demonstration for the benefit of all the Light Workers in the audience who were from the Planet Earth. Thus, graphically showing us how very difficult it will be for us to shed our dense, earthbound bodies. Indicating that it will indeed take dedicated effort to regain our multidimensional light bodies.

EVACUATION AND ASCENSION VISION

Another very vivid vision was shown to me one morning a few days after transmission of the Lessons began. This vision had a great impact upon my consciousness. I'll just describe it in as much detail as possible so that perhaps you can visualize the scene and share this memory with me. The Masters want me to share this with you as a visual aid to help all to accept the inevitable reality of the final cleansing of Mother Earth and the part that all her inhabitants will be compelled to play.

In the vision, there suddenly appeared a multitude or ordinary people walking along the trafficway which was strangely clear of traffic. This was a mass movement of humanity filling the breadth and width of the trafficway. Coming from the west and moving toward the east. They were walking peacefully along. Their arms were relaxed and empty as though each had simply discontinued what they had been doing and walked off their jobs at some prearranged signal. It appeared that all walks of life were represented. Each person was following their own inner guidance and seemed unaware that they were part of a multitude. There was no pushing or shoving. No laughing or joking. Just smooth forward motion to some appointed destination. I'm reminded of the hymn; "Just As I Am Without One Plea."

In similar fashion, another multitude appeared coming from the south, moving toward the north and joined the first group as they intersected on the trafficway. It was then that I seemed to join them. We proceeded some distance down the road. No one complained of being hungry or thirsty. We seemed to be tireless though we had not eaten or had anything to drink. There seemed to pervade a feeling of calm expectancy.

The group slowed to a stop as we approached a very broad, magnificent set of steps that were radiant and had a sparkling clean glow. Architecturally, you would find steps such as these at the entrance of stately government buildings, ancient libraries or museums. But none of this world's buildings could compare to the indescribable beauty that was before us. These steps seemed several stories high and could easily accommodate the assembled multitudes. They led to and terminated at two magnificent golden doors.

The two golden doors opened wide. The several tall radiant men who appeared to be leading the group, walked through the open doors. The doors closed behind them, but the crowd was not dismayed. It was as though each of us had every confidence that those doors would open again in a very short time and we would be admitted when it was our time to enter through those gates.

"Blessed are they that do his commandments, that they may have right to the Tree of Life, and may enter in through the gates into the city." Revelations 22: 14

Could this vision be a preview of things to come? The Ascended Masters offer these Lessons to all of us who will apply ourselves and set aside a few minutes twice each day to attain our spiritual evolution. The Lessons are a rare gift of Love from the Ascended Masters. This is an opportunity that has been afforded each of us for the mere acceptance and daily practice of prayer and meditation focusing on Unconditional Love and Unconditional Forgiveness. Telepathic communications from the Universe, Channeling, Multidimensional Experiences, Manifesting your needs are the possible rewards for your willingness to help yourself and mankind welcome in the Millennium.

"Ask and it shall be given to you.
Seek and ye shall find.
Knock and the door shall be opened to you."

LIGHT WORKERS CHANNELING

CHANNELED POETRY FOR BETTY HUDSON BY SYLVIA HUGHEY AT LAKE WAUKOMIS, MO. August 19, 1994

Sylvia Hughey is truely a Light Worker and a very dear friend of mine. Sylvia has received inspired poems for 25 years and is an ardent student of Unity Teaching. She is a Graphologist and Paranormal Investigator. Most notably, Sylvia is a Healer working with the Universal Life Energy using the Usui System combined with color healing.

BIRTH OF DIVINITY

You are giving birth to a New Vision -
A very slow, yet rapidly proceeding and painful cycle.

Stay firm, stay steady, be true to yourself
It is in honoring your own identity -
The birthing time shall pass.

The love of the ages holds you safe
and close within its bosom.
Follow your heart of hearts
It is in wavering your power dissipates.

Remain grounded in your Faith, Dear One.
You have all power of the universe available to you.

Again, be true to yourself.
You then honor the Divineness of yourself.

Blessings, Sylvia

CHANNELED READINGS BY REVEREND FERN MORELAND

March 16, 1994, Kansas City Psychic, Reverend Fern Moreland called me one evening and asked if she could come over since she had just received two messages for me. The following channeled messages are what she felt I might find interesting and could be important. I was quite mystified at the time. Some parts certainly have taken place.

As we come to you Betty, we wonder about things too. Your heart is not in a stew. There are many good things coming your way, don't you see. You are coming into a different vibration - we're feeling that around thee. New changes, new laws, new good things you see. You're wondering about life and what it will bring thee.

In 1994 we show a lot of people around and they want to know. The teaching end of Astrology and another school will be opening around you. You have many things to impart don't you see and more — you want to know about Spirituality. "What can I teach people" you say, "besides the stars?" The spirits are saying where they are and where is life teaching them and bringing them along the plan? Where are they going and where have they been? And what lane of existence are they in - don't you know. What road are they going? Is it hard to hoe? No, you'll teach many things and your philosophy because that's really the way with thee. You sound things out and you listen to them too and see if you can channel it in a different way too.

Oh, you want to do many things. All the fingers are in many pies and you're going to lick each one to see what you can see. But you have many things a brewin' and you try to get yourself a stewin'! Too little time for what I should know - too little time in the future you know. The changes in the world are keepin' me stirred up and what am I doin' — I'm just a young pup. I'm doing the knowledge that I've done before. Taught this is one lifetime -if not four. I'm going to teach people in a different way too. None of that mundane stuff - what's that to you. We'll teach you in the philosophies in the far away land, here, in the way that we can beat the band. They're the leaders of the world, don't you see, not this little tiny stuff. That's not the way with thee. More of the higher and broader existences now that you know and if you don't know it - you'll travel, just so. So what am I doing with this world now? Well, you'll be surprised what I do, anyhow.

I've come a long way like Virginia Slims, you see. And, I'm coming in a different pattern and a different ecstasy. I look at life as a yearning and a learning tool, you know. I'm going to teach in the future and, this I do know. And when I say future, I'm talking in eons. We are not talking about the next year or three. We have many things to impart to the world and we send people back with all in the mind in a whirl. But each time an existence comes around, you too, are going to advance maybe a notch or two. But you are going to teach from the higher learning, you see. Why should you go back to kindergarten, when you are in grade three! You are coming from a different dimension and times we show true. We'll send you at times in the dream world around you - you'll wonder and wonder, "Now why am I here and why am I bending your ear?

I am the future and I talk to you too. And my name? We'll let you figure too. And when I come from existence that goes beyond this time, I'm speaking to you, my dear, in a different rhyme. Some say Sananda and Jesus, you know - some say there's Ashtar around you too - or, maybe, just so. But what about those from a different Galaxy and many with thee?

You're one to work in the computer world too because that's communication that will come around you. Sit there at times.

Write to us, you know. We've been trying to get through to you from a long time ago. But sometime you drum and you hum - just away. But, what are you doing? We have our way.

Watch Betty, watch out in 1994. We're going to speak to you in different patterns than we have before. Maybe a trance. You go this and there we're going to work on you from a different air. We're coming from a different Galaxy and maybe two, you see. How many Galaxies are there and how many around you? Sure you are wondering and wondering, just what you can see?

Think Betty, think all around thee. We have dozens of ways we talk to you too and you've heard - oh, you've heard us before - long, long before. But now as we come around you once more, you watch your writing in 1994.

GREAT WHITE FEATHER CHANNELED BY FERN MORELAND FOR BETTY HUDSON

In the ways of life were glowing, we send our love to you - We know you like this tune, we'll sing it right back to you.

As we come to you Betty and many things here - we're going to talk to you a little bit for you to hear - with this sore throat that Fern has - we'll get it out - we'll have our say.

You are doing many things through the Spirit that's true and this next new year is a new pathway for you. "What am I doing and where do I go?" Spirits say there are three places for you to go. You're going to tread many waters too and wonder, "Is this for me to do?" Oh yes we say - not spiritual water, you know ' you're going to go where God sends you - just so!

And you worry about your family, you see - but not to worry about. They're going to come closer to thee. You'll say "No that can't be for my son is where he is at." Spirits are saying - "He'll move at the drop of a hat!"

You're also going to work with other people too. It can be like the children of the light family around you. As you work with Sananda there's another spirit guide - the spirits are saying - he's always by your side. There are several spirits you talk to you know, and they're the kind that really makes your heart glow.

So, what are you going to do for the future - we see - oh, there's much, much more to your spirituality. There's going to be a reckoning of time with you too, and you'll say, "I'm going to do some things for me too!" God will send you to where you'll go for your recreation, you see, and you'll find much pleasure in nature around thee. You're going to find more places that you've not heard of, you know with the spirits until your heart glows.

You'll learn to walk and work through nature, we say. You'll not do much with the Ascension until it is that day. You're going to get yourself ready for your own existence, too. And work with the Spirituality as God shines around you. There's more and more things coming than what we know on earth. The spirits are saying, "We're giving you a new birth." We're giving you a way of expanding yourself too.

Oh, you're going to settle down and do less for you than right now - what is doing for the spirit, you say. You're not going to wear yourself out - we won't let you have that way.

We are going to let you settle in a different way you see that can relax you and work with you and heal yourself, too. A healer you are - now don't you see.

Who is that person from the planet they're told that he comes from. He is a person from a long time of old. You've worked with the Old Ones from the spirits, we see. You've worked with the healings, that's the way with thee. You may have your troubles and your heart troubles too, but did you every stop to think, you could heal that too? And then when you get yourself in your stride - stand straight up and lift your arms to the heaven. That's the way and then when you stretch yourself to the stars, call upon the people who have worked with you before and they'll reel their names out to you - much, much more than before!

You'll work with three (3) planets of a different Galaxy. You're going to work through the healers - that's what's coming around thee.

You'll sing your songs - oh, yes you will. Because, we love to hear your trill. We know that there are many things coming, too, that'll work and work through the earth around you.

Why do you worry about things here, you see. Yes, you worry a bit, but that's the way with thee. We're going to send you much power, you know. You say "Naw, this is not just so." But when you come to think of yourself as a Virgoan too - don't you know - you're Earthbound. You are earth - here is you. But you're also another earth in a higher time too that you will work with this galaxy that is much, much like thee. You're going to find others as they come to your door. Are they from earth - are they from the terrestrial part of earth? Are they from the extraterrestrial part of earth? Where are they from and why are they here? Stop and think - it's an Angel - unaware here. You are going to entertain the celestial beings too. And you'll wonder - aren't they a little like me? Like you?

Well, we'll say many things to you Betty, because that's the way it is. And you're going to do many things kinda like showbiz. You show yourself off and we'll show you proud and true. Are you not that Virgoan? Well, that's the way it is with you! You come from a higher plane, now don't you see, with an analytical mind - what can we say - that's the way it is with thee. You analyze everything around you like a science bug too. But, you're going to work much more for the being in you.

You can teach, you can teach - oh - we say that again and again. There are many things that you can teach and really raise a din. Not always Astrology, you know. There are many ways of teaching. That's the way to go! You can also work through the music there too. Sing your songs and write the music - yes, you can do that too! Put your paintings down and draw as you've never drawn before. The spirits say more talents are coming than ever have been before. You'll feel yourself expanding yourself and saying, "Well, I'd like to slow down a bit, too!" But, what is "slow down?" S-l-o-w, maybe - that too! So, as you travel this world, you see - Astral Project Yourself and We'll Be There For Thee!

GLOSSARY

ASCENDED MASTERS—People who reached a high degree of spirituality before they left the Earth plane and thereby ascended into higher dimensions.

ASHTAR—Supreme Commander of the Extraterrestrials and second-in-command to Sananda, Jesus the Christ. He volunteered eons ago to serve Sananda. Ashtar is Lord of the Planet Venus.

AURA—Electromagnetically charged energy surrounding each inhabitant on Earth.

BROTHERHOOD OF LIGHT—A federation of Ascended Masters, both male and female. Sometimes referred to as the Great White Brotherhood. No racial or gender is implied. The members include ascended females and males and they are androgynous. White is indicative of White Light.

CHAKRAS—The etheric body's sense organs that appear to rotate as vortices and are only visible to clairvoyants. Most humans use seven chakras of the ten we are reported to have and each vibrates at the frequency of the seven colors that combine as the White Light.

FAMILY OF LIGHT, LIGHTWORKERS, STARSEEDS—

Humans who are on the path of spiritual enlightenment and transformation. And, volunteered eons ago to incarnate on the Earth plane to experience living in a dense body to gain an understanding of how to help the Masters with the transformation of Mother Earth and her inhabitants.

ELDERS—Highly evolved Beings, revered and respected for their wisdom and spiritual knowledge who have ascended into higher realms and frequencies.

GOLDEN PYRAMID—Visualization of a Golden Pyramid during Sananda's New Meditation can connect the biomagnetic body, the planetary body, and the interplanetary body with higher evolutionary orders for Divine Wisdom.

KUTHUMI—An ascended Master who has served Sananda and is known to have been the teacher who instructed young Jesus. He has been reported to have incarnated as Pythagoras, St. Francis of Assisi, the Master who built the Taj Mahal and John the Beloved.

LOVE—An electromagnetic force that creates and encompasses everything. God is love and creates life.

MASTERS—Spiritually evolved men and women whose frequencies transcend other human beings and assist in ruling the world.

MERKABAH—Masters use this light energy vehicle to reach the spiritually evolved in their multidimensional mind circumventing time and space between various universes.

MULTIDIMENSIONAL—As the Pole Shift progresses, the vibrational frequencies of the earth are shifting from the earth's 3rd dimensional resonances to 4th dimensional frequencies.

MULTIDIMENSIONAL MIND—Attained through right living and right thinking, prayer and meditation.

NEW AGE—The age of seeking spirituality and oneness for the millennium that is approaching with the Second Coming of Christ.

PLANET—A heavenly body that can be part of our Solar system or part of the many galaxies in the Universe.

SANANDA—An Ascended Master who is Jesus, the Christ, and the Supreme Commander of Planet Earth and the millions of volunteers who have come to assist Mother Earth.

SOUL CHAKRA (Higher Self)—The 8th Chakra is the Soul Chakra working entirely in the etheric body and connects the aura and psychic energies. It contains your genetic makeup, known as the Akashic Records, endowing you with telepathic communication with other dimensions.

TERRA—Another name for Mother Earth.

THIRD EYE—The 6th Chakra, located between the eyebrows, activated through prayer and meditation. The seat of clairvoyance.

TONING—Specific resonances that activate the chakras produced through verbal sounding and tones.

VIBRATIONAL FREQUENCY—Atoms and sub-particles of every living thing or object vibrate at specific frequencies. The higher the frequency, the closer to the Light.

UNCONDITIONAL LOVE